Sutton Coldfield College

D0228005

Discard

Deve...tive
Training Skills

Dr Tony Pont is a management development consultant and graduate of the Universities of Leeds and Bradford.

He has held appointments in Higher Education and in industry. In the 1980's he obtained a Fulbright Exchange Award to the USA.

He has extensive international experience in Europe, USA, the Middle East and SE Asia. He has undertaken assignments with clients in the public sector, pharmaceuticals, oil and gas, construction, automobiles, retailing and financial services. He is currently a visiting faculty member at a number of Business Schools in the UK working on qualification programmes such as the MBA, and a Director of a HRD consultancy, based in Northamptonshire.

His consultancy, AP international, offers a range of training and development services, especially management training courses, management development consultancy, psychometric testing and counselling services. Tony can be contacted by telephone on +44(0)1327 342339; by e mail at A.M.Pont@btinternet.com and through AP International's website at www.apinternational.co.uk

For Leslie Rupert, who would have appreciated the effort.

The Chartered Institute of Personnel and Development is the leading publisher of books and reports for personnel and training professionals, students, and all those concerned with the effective management and development of people at work. For details of all our titles, please contact the publishing department:

tel: 020-8263 3387

fax: 020-8263 3850

e-mail: publish@cipd.co.uk

The catalogue of all CIPD titles can be viewed on the CIPD website:

www.cipd.co.uk/bookstore

Developing Effective Training Skills

Tony Pont

The Chartered Institute of Personnel and Development

Published by the Chartered Institute of Personnel and Development, CIPD House,
Camp Road, London, SW19 4UX

Previously published by McGrawhill (1991, 1996)
First published by the CIPD 2003

© Chartered Institute of Personnel and Development, 2003

All rights reserved. No part of this publication may be reproduced, stored in a retrieval
system, or transmitted, in any form or by any means, electronic, mechanical,
photocopying, recording, or otherwise, without the prior written permission of the
publisher.

This publication may not be sold, lent, hired out or otherwise dealt with in the course
of trade or supplied in any form of binding or cover other than that in which it is
published without the prior written permission of the publisher.

No responsibility for loss occasioned to any person acting or refraining from action as
a result of any material in this publication can be accepted by the editor, author or
publisher.

Design by Beacon GDT, Mitcheldean, Gloucestershire
Typeset by Fakenham Photosetting Ltd, Fakenham, Norfolk
Printed in Great Britain by The Cromwell Press, Trowbridge, Wiltshire

British Library Cataloguing in Publication Data
A catalogue of this publication is available from the British Library

ISBN 1 84398 027 4

The views expressed in this publication are the author's own and may not necessarily
reflect those of the CIPD.

The CIPD has made every effort to trace and acknowledge copyright holders. If any
source has been overlooked, CIPD Enterprises Ltd would be pleased to redress this for
future editions.

Sutton Coldfield
College LRC
Sutton Campus

Accession

94262

Class

658.3124
PON

Chartered Institute of Personnel and Development, CIPD House,
Camp Road, London, SW19 4UX
Tel: 020 8971 9000   Fax: 020 8263 3333   Email: cipd@cipd.co.uk
Email: cipd@cipd.co.uk   Website: www.cipd.co.uk
Incorporated by Royal Charter.   Registered Charity No. 1079797

■ CONTENTS

■ LIST OF FIGURES/TABLES

█ FIGURES

TABLES

■ PREFACE

George Bernard Shaw once wrote `He who can, does. He who cannot, teaches.' For those who have tried, there is a sudden realisation that teaching is not as easy as first thought. It is not merely a question of standing in front of an audience and casting one's pearls.

For those who have been involved in the teaching of adults there is an immediate realisation of the difficulty of this challenge. At the same time there is a quick understanding of the enormous satisfaction and stimulation that one can enjoy when the process is carried out professionally.

In today's rapidly changing world the need for training is of greater importance. The days when an individual learned skills under apprenticeship, articles, professional training, etc., that were to equip that individual with a job for life have long since gone. Learning is now a lifelong process and is necessary not just for personal growth and development, but merely to stand still. Old clichés such as `cradle to grave', `womb to tomb', have never been more relevant to personal development and occupational competence and success.

Organisations as well as their people are now beginning to become proactive in this process. Awareness is beginning to be translated into action and commitment. Large organisations have developed their own training and leadership and management development programmes, and many smaller ones have formed networks or consortiums to help meet training needs and finance delivery. The number of managers who are undertaking and completing programmes leading to qualifications such as Certificate, Diploma and Masters degree is increasing annually.

At the same time, our knowledge and understanding of the adult learning process has increased enormously in recent years. This is being reflected in change from the traditional methods of business education and training. Today the emphasis is moving away from the teaching to the learning, from the tutor to the learner. The emphasis in the training methods adopted and the responsibility for the learning rests very firmly with the learner. The late Winston Churchill's observation, made many years ago, that `I love to learn but I hate being taught' has at last been acknowledged.

It is against this background of changing attitudes, knowledge and methods that in 1989 I produced the manuscript for the first edition of this book. I said then that the number of people who will be involved in training and development in the years ahead will increase as provision widens and increases, and that prediction has proved correct. The trend for increasing involvement of line managers in training and development, and the increase in the number of informal training and development opportunities in the workplace has accelerated this trend. For those suddenly thrown in at the deep end it can be a traumatic experience. I hope that the content of this book will help reduce the trauma, the period of `trial and error' learning and will help people develop their training skills.

While this edition is again largely targeted at the inexperienced trainer who is starting a career in training and development, it is also aimed at the more experienced trainer who may need to consider alternative ideas and approaches. Since I wrote the 2nd edition in 1995, there have been many changes or developments that have impacted directly on training. The most obvious is the electronic revolution that has spawned the internet, email and the growth in the ownership and use of PC's. Whilst these will never replace the more traditional forms of training, their presence, potential and impact on training cannot be ignored, and they offer some exciting alternative options. Consequently, sections on E-learning and the use of graphics packages in oral presentations have been added at appropriate places within the book.

This section, along with other new sections, has been written in response to changes in training and development which have taken place in the past eight years and also in response to the feedback I have received on the first two editions from readers and reviewers. This has come from around the world and has been constructive, helpful and encouraging. A very sincere thanks to everyone who contributed, and I hope that this edition will encourage similar feedback.

One of the great appeals of the first two editions was, according to the feedback and reviews, its simplicity and practical application. While I have introduced some new theories and concepts, I hope the same comments still apply. There is a fine line between striving for academic credibility and achieving practical relevance, and I hope I have not fallen between the two stools.

The book should also serve as a course text and as a launching pad for those undertaking serious study for a qualification in training and development. It should be a useful text for those taking a Certificate or Diploma in Training and Development (and in the UK, NVQ Levels 3–5), while for those aspiring higher, the expanded Further Reading section at the end of each chapter will provide a starting point for those who want to study and practice in greater depth in the relevant field. These sections have also been updated to reflect new publications in the past eight years.

As before, I cannot complete the introduction without a few words of thanks to so many people who have shared their views and experience with me, and also helped, supported and influenced my thinking during my career. They are too numerous to mention by name, but special thanks are due to:

- the numerous adult students and managers who have attended programmes with which I have been involved in Europe, the USA, the Middle East and South East Asia;

- Brian Hirst, formerly Head of Business and Management Studies at Keighley Technical College, who first stressed to me that education is for the benefit of the learner;

- Merle E. Peacock, Jnr, Superintendent of Schools, MSAD No. 11, Gardiner, Maine, USA, and the School Board, for opening the door to a once-in-a-lifetime opportunity. The experience will never be forgotten;

- Malcolm S. Knowles, who in one day in San Antonio, Texas, made me stop and think at greater length about adult learning and who started me on a continual process of self-directed inquiry;

- Dave Francis, friend and colleague, for sharing his philosophy and expertise with me on numerous management development programmes;

- The late Roger Bennett, without whose encouragement and support, I would never have started out as a writer;

- Gillian Pont for over 30 years of support, and for acting as a constant sounding board for ideas;

- Simon and Nicholas Pont who continue to test my ideas as well as providing a valuable source of feedback.

The responsibility for the ideas expressed rests entirely with me, and while these ideas might provoke disagreement, my sincere wish is that they provoke thought and lead to a development of training skills. By developing these, your own development as a trainer and the personal development of your learners should be greatly enhanced. Good luck in your training and development activities!

1 ■ THE TRAINING FIELD – WHAT IT IS

Training is about developing people as individuals and helping them to become more confident and competent in their lives and in their jobs. The learning process is at the core of training and the ways of, and opportunities for, learning are numerous and varied. After reading this chapter you will:

- have a wider understanding of why training is becoming more important in our society
- be familiar with the five stages of the training cycle, and the key components of each stage
- know the main types of training
- be able to list many of the roles of the trainer
- have recognised that much of training is about facilitating the learning of others.

The training field is a rapidly growing sector of our lives and has come of age as a profession. The need for training has always been present in every walk of life, but today the need is so much greater. There are many reasons for this, but the most important are probably:

- the pace of change
- the attitude of employers
- the attitude of individuals.

The pace of change

The pace of change is increasingly gathering momentum. What was appropriate 10 years ago is no longer appropriate today. Indeed, in some areas of our lives what was appropriate last month is no longer appropriate today. This is very different from the experience of previous generations.

Until the turn of the twentieth century (see Figure 1), the time-span of social change extended over several generations. A person did not expect to have to cope with any significant change over a lifetime, but if there was change, the change would be gradual.

Today with each successive generation we can expect several periods of change and we must cope with them at a faster rate of imposition. The pace of change is accelerating. Under these conditions the knowledge and skills gained in yesteryear will no longer be sufficient to equip a person for a lifetime. They are appropriate for only a short period of time before becoming obsolete.

The modernday workplace has changed beyond recognition in the past 40 years. In the past, employees could reasonably expect to be employed by the same organisation for their entire working lives. 'Jobs for life' were the norm, and the skill set needed to perform a job rarely needed updating. However, the combination of recessions, globalisation and changing technology has altered the way we live our lives and earn our living. Today, most of the workforce expect to work for many different organisations before retirement, and possibly to have three or four different careers. Employees expect jobs to change to keep up with developments in technology, legislation, management practices and organisational restructuring. The days of needing one skill for a working life have gone, to be replaced by the need to be multi-skilled. Employees also need to show evidence to future employers of their commitment to their own professional development in order to maintain their marketability.

To illustrate the pace of change, let us consider the changes that have taken place in the period between preparing the manuscript for the 1st edition of this book (1989) and preparing the manuscript for its 3rd edition (2003).

Figure 1 The relationship of the time-span of social change to individual life-span

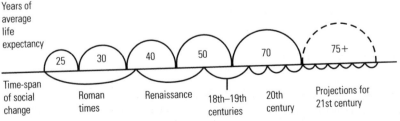

- In 1989 the Berlin Wall was still standing and Eastern Europe lived under totalitarian dictatorships. By 2003 many of the former Eastern-bloc countries had become members of NATO and the EU.

- In 1989 the East and West had massive nuclear arsenals pointed at each other. In 2003 their intelligence services mounted a joint operation to prevent a missile falling into the hands of terrorists.

- In 1989 inflation and double-digit interest rates had been a fact of life for three decades, and high unemployment for 15 years. By 2003 inflation had been under control for a decade, interest rates were at a 50-year low and businesses were struggling to fill staff vacancies.

- In 1989 mobile phones were the size of bricks and rarely seen outside the City. In 2003 they were the size of a matchbox and used by almost every teenager in the country.

- Many words and expressions we hadn't heard in 1989 had entered the popular vocabulary by 2003, including: 'e-mail', 'text message', 'spin', '9/11'.

More recent developments were described on both sides of the Atlantic in 2003. Speaking at the Annual Conference of the ASTD in San Diego in May, President and Chief Executive Tina Sung said the events of 11 September 2001 marked the shift from 'new economy' prosperity to 'next economy' uncertainty and slowdown. Training will be expected to do more for less. It will continue to be of the same importance, but cycles will get shorter and faster-paced as businesses struggle to survive. Training will have to be closely linked to business strategy. Three trends were becoming evident:

- an increased interest in evaluating training and the return on investment

- e-learning reaching record levels while classroom learning has declined – In 2002 the proportion of companies delivering training via learning technologies rose from around 8.5 per cent in 2001 to 10.1 per cent, while classroom training dropped slightly from 79.4 per cent to 77.1 per cent. E-learning has become the most important trend to affect the US professions in 50 years, and because of the economies of scale that can be achieved through this medium, it will continue to grow in popularity.

- a renewed interest by companies in leadership development and coaching.

In the UK, the fifth report of the CIPD annual training and development survey in 2003 outlined a number of changes to the training profession in recent years. These included:

- Training methods were becoming more sophisticated and were incorporating the latest technology. There has been a decline in the dominance of the classroom and an increase in the range of methods used by trainers.

- Courses were giving way to more bespoke training, and training was becoming more closely integrated with the organisation's agenda.

- Senior managers were taking training more seriously and line managers were more involved in its delivery and offering learners more significant support.

- Workplace diversity training was a key topic, with 58 per cent of organisations providing it. Gender, ethnic status and disability were the main issues.

- There was economic downturn in the private sector and continuing funding restraints in the public sector, but despite the gloomy backdrop, training spending in both sectors was relatively resilient.

Such enormous changes at all levels must impact upon the daily lives of individuals and organisations. We must therefore develop a training strategy backed by training systems that equip and empower individuals to cope with change. We need to move away from traditional methods of transmitting knowledge to helping people to learn how to learn. The emphasis should change from *what* – ie what knowledge or skill do we impart? – to *how* – ie how do we help people to learn, to ask questions and to acquire the skills of self-directed enquiry?

The attitude of employers

The attitude of employers to training is changing. Although there are still many employers who see it as an expensive overhead (and the first thing that accountants cut back on when times are hard), many now recognise that training is an investment and not a cost. The awareness in management development, generated in the 1980s in the UK by the reports of Coopers & Lybrand, Constable & McCormick, and Handy, is at long last beginning to be translated into commitment. The implications of the quotation 'If you think training is expensive, try ignorance!' are beginning to be realised and acted upon. Michael Porter's report (2003) advocates an increased investment in education if the UK is to increase the skills, innovation and enterprise of its workforce.

The attitude of individuals

The attitude of individuals to personal development is changing. We have begun to realise that training and development are lifelong processes, that the ability to learn does not necessarily decline sharply with age, that our potential could be limitless, and that personal development is important for both individual growth and occupational success.

Many employers are becoming aware of this shift in individual attitudes. Nowhere is this more evident than among the generation born in the 1960s, dubbed 'Generation X' in the American novel of the same name written by Douglas Coupland. This new generation frequently views personal development as more important than money, power, or even comfort at work. Professor John Hunt of the London Business School, in an extensive research project with a sample of over 20,000 managers, found that attitudes among managers had changed in the past two decades. Whereas in the 1970s power was the most important motivator, in the 1990s autonomy and independence had risen in importance, with the acquisition of new skills of great importance among 'Generation X'.

Against this backdrop of change at the individual, organisational and societal level is an evolution of the training provision required to meet conflicting interests. Employers and employees are wanting a full return on their investment, the former – particularly if they are footing the bill – seeking added value and bottom-line results. The types of training on offer can be grouped as follows:

- *Technical and vocational training* – This involves a heavy emphasis on skills or competencies. In the UK this type of training, backed often by government funding and linked to qualification routes (GNVQ or NVQ-General and National Vocational Qualifications), has expanded rapidly in an attempt to meet skills shortages. Management training has also become more competency based, often linking into the NVQ framework. In the business school world, employers are having an increasing influence on content, with the result that many qualification programmes (Certificate, Diploma, Masters degree) have a work-related project as part of the assessed programme, which gives the employer the chance to implement some of the recommendations of the project report.

- *Personal development programmes* – The demand for these programmes has grown considerably, courses abounding in such areas as stress management, assertiveness training, women in management, creative problem-solving, teamworking, etc, in addition to the more standard range of management skills programmes. Individuals are also looking for added value and, in addition to valuable insights into self and personal development, are seeking to use the courses attended to build up a portfolio of evidence to obtain 'credits' towards a recognised qualification. As a result, academic institutions are becoming more flexible in their assessment procedures.

With the growth in the training market, training is now available from a variety of sources. Large organisations provide their own, and some companies form consortiums to widen their provision. In addition, there are numerous public and private educational institutions, professional associations, consultancies, home study, television and other media. All these providers offer a variety of approaches which must be matched to the needs of the individual and the organisation.

The goal of all these media should be to provide individual satisfaction and development so that the employing organisation can also benefit. The more that people can broaden their knowledge of the training function – particularly through the variety of techniques available –the more likely they are to give satisfaction. That should also increase competence and confidence, and result in personal growth.

THE CONTRIBUTION OF TRAINING TO THE BUSINESS

Trainers must be aware of the close relationship between training and profit. Training for the sake of training is not the order of the day. For training personnel to make a case to senior management for a bigger slice of the cake, they will have to show that training achieves tangible bottom-line results. Senior decision-makers must be made to view training as an investment – training is needed not only to create a skilled workforce but also to maintain the high level of skills demanded by the constantly changing workplace and to equip people to meet future demands.

In order to add value to the business, training should accord with the direction of the corporate and business strategy – information which should cascade down the organisation from senior management. Training provision should therefore help meet the business needs. This is represented diagrammatically in Figure 2. Trainers must use every opportunity to give feedback on success, particularly upon the impact on the business, to senior management.

Figure 2   The relationship between business needs and training provision

In the UK the Investors in People (IiP) award, which was launched in 1991, requires an organisation to make and demonstrate a commitment from the top to develop its people in order to achieve its business objectives. In the first three years of its existence, about 11,000 organisations committed themselves to achieving the national standard. If the training provision is not delivered professionally, the quality of learning suffers, with the strong possibility that individual competence in the workplace may fall – with adverse effects upon business performance. Much of the content of this book is aimed at helping the trainer to be more professional and competent at up-front training so that the benefits to participants, and ultimately to the business, are maximised.

THE TRAINING CYCLE

Training can be viewed as a cyclical process which is ongoing. There are five distinct phases in the cycle, each of which logically follows on from the previous stage:

1   analysing training needs

2   planning and designing the training approach

3   developing the training materials

4   delivering the training

5   evaluating the training.

The evaluation stage not only cycles back into Stage 1 but also cycles back into the other three. Evaluation must be an ongoing process if training product and performance are to be refined and improved (see Figure 3).

Figure 3 The training cycle

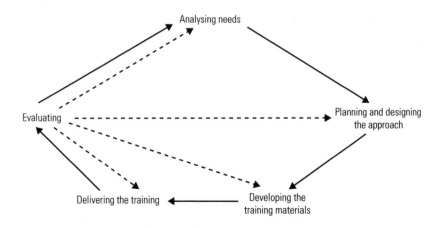

Let us look at the five stages in the cycle in a little more detail.

Analysing training needs

There are three main areas in which this analysis may take place:

- *needs at organisational level* – Where in the organisation is training most needed?

- *needs at occupational level* – What is needed in terms of skill, knowledge and attitude so that the duties of various jobs can be effectively and competently carried out? This is the process of job analysis.

- *needs at individual level* – Who needs training in what? What is needed by individuals to bridge the competency gap between where they are now and where they should be in terms of skill, knowledge and attitude? This is the process of needs assessment.

The exact relative importance of the three areas will vary from situation to situation, but the final stage will always involve an identification of the people to be trained and the competency gap to be bridged.

Planning and designing the training approach

As in the analysis stage, a great deal of information gathering is required, particularly if you are involved with a new programme. It is also worth spending plenty of time on this phase. There is often a tendency to skate over the planning and rush into some sort of action.

The importance of planning cannot be overemphasised: 'Failing to plan is planning to fail.' The time invested in good planning will reap benefits later in the cycle.

Among the tasks that have to be addressed in this phase are:

- defining the learning objectives of the training
- deciding on the most appropriate methods of training
- deciding on the staffing and support
- selecting from the variety of media
- deciding upon content
- identifying evaluation tools

- deciding on prerequisites and pre-course preparation for the learners
- organising and sequencing the training.

Developing the training materials

This is the stage when the work of the two previous stages is integrated into a complete set of materials to assist course delivery and meet the stated learning objectives. The most time-consuming part of the cycle, particularly when developing or customising a course, it will take up less time than the delivery stage only with a course that has run many times.

Among the training materials that must be developed and assembled are:

- course outlines
- session plans
- learner materials – workbooks, reading, handouts, etc
- audio-visual aids – OHP transparencies, films, flipcharts, etc
- evaluation sheets.

Other important activities have to be carried out during this stage:

- background reading so that one is up to date on the subject
- reviewing existing materials and altering or replacing them
- briefing the tutors
- fitting individual training sessions into a logical sequence so that it all hangs together, which, with a new course, may require several trial-and-error runs
- taking care of all the administrative arrangements, etc – for example, booking a venue, and such administrative details as preparing joining instructions
- validating new materials – for example, films and/or videos – before the event.

Delivering the training

This is the stage when (hopefully!) it all comes together. If the planning and preparation have been thorough, the chances of success are vastly increased.

With the advent of participatory methods, the role of the trainer has extended well beyond merely presenting. Facilitating, motivating, inspiring, leading, co-ordinating, managing and evaluating are just a few of the many roles that will be required.

Evaluating the training

This is an often neglected but vitally important part of the cycle. It involves some evaluation of:

- self – via self-analysis, evaluation forms and feedback from colleagues in the training team. Could you have done better? Are there areas for improvement?

- the course materials – Do they need replacing, revising, updating?

- the whole course – self, learners, observers

- individual parts of the course – self, learners, observers

- the situation after the course – via a follow-up inquiry seeking to measure improved performance or behaviour in the work situation. How effective has the transfer of learning been to the real world? This stage ceases only when the course is no longer relevant.

These five stages help to bring about a change in the delegates' behaviour. This change is called *learning*, and without it there has been no effective training.

TYPES OF TRAINING

There are two broad categories of training:

- *trainer-controlled training* – a good example is the lecture

- *learner-controlled training* – a good example would be a distance-learning package; another would be a mature Action Learning set who receive very little help or advice from the facilitator.

All learning is essentially the responsibility of the learners. The more they put into the experience, the more they tend to get out of it. This applies to the whole range of learning opportunities that are available from a lecture (did the learners concentrate and listen?) to the participatory methods (did they prepare and risk themselves?) to everyday learning opportunities (were they aware of the situation and did they evaluate what was observed and experienced?). Very often learning is consolidated and integrated following a period of contemplation and implementation, which requires commitment.

The main types of training may be summarised as follows.

Classroom

The classroom approach can vary greatly, from the traditional method in which the trainer adopts the role of lecturer with little or no student participation, to where the trainer adopts the role of facilitator and the style ranges from non-directive to directive.

A classroom situation in which the emphasis is on learner participation certainly produces greater learner enjoyment and, usually, more effective learning.

Outdoors

This form of training has been widely used for a number of years and has probably been most used by the armed forces, particularly in such fields as leadership training and team building. An increasing number of companies are now using such an approach.

It has many recommendations, not least that it requires a whole-hearted commitment, and that individual defences are quickly lowered and barriers to learning are removed in a very non-structured environment.

Some writers might argue that it lacks the academic rigour of classroom training, but if it is linked meaningfully with classroom input and debriefing a great deal of effective learning and development can take place.

Computer-assisted learning

This is largely a refinement of programmed learning in which individuals work through written material in a programmed way. Learners progress in a step-by-step fashion, having received feedback on their responses.

Such programmed learning has become more sophisticated in recent years with the advent of computers, videos and CD-ROMs/DVDs. Individuals can work at home if they have their own PC, or on a workstation at work which may form part of an open learning facility.

One of the great advantages of such training is flexibility – the learners can progress at their own pace and wherever they want. The disadvantages are isolation, which can result in low motivation and reduced commitment, and cost. The hardware and software for some of the interactive video packages on the market can cost several thousand pounds. A detailed cost/benefit analysis is required before an investment of such magnitude is undertaken.

E-learning

With the growth of the World Wide Web and the increasing use of computers at home and in the workplace, e-learning has been the most significant development in the training field during the past decade.

E-learning comprises a wide variety of specialist technologies, although they all have one thing in common – delivery by electronic methods. These include, but are not limited to, the Internet, intranets and CD-ROMs.

Like computer-assisted learning, it offers many advantages such as instant access and economies of scale ... but many of the disadvantages of distance learning apply.

For the trainer, it presents many more challenges in its design and delivery, not least keeping up to date with technological developments and maintaining IT competence. Nevertheless, its potential is enormous, particularly when it is blended with other methods of training.

Simulation

This type of training is very participative and is used mainly for skills training. It may reinforce other types of training – for example, classroom training.

As far as possible simulation training is linked to the real world. Good examples are in-tray exercises, which are used to train managers in decision-making, and role-play as part of an assessment centre – a method increasingly used in managerial selection.

Another good example is flight simulation, which is a realistic imitation of the real world. This trains pilots in flying skills and also teaches them to deal with emergencies on the aircraft.

Training methods

Within the types of training, some flexibility exists as to the methods used. These are examined in detail later in this book. Equally, within the methods a variety of media can be used – overhead projectors, flipcharts, films, slides, etc – which can enhance the method of delivery. These are also examined later in the book.

As a general rule, try to aim for variety in both method and media – it breaks up the learner's day and allows the message to get through on more than one channel.

THE ROLE OF THE TRAINER

The obvious role of the trainer is as a *deliverer*, so the key competency to acquire is *presenting*. A trainer should be good at presenting information so that the attention of the audience is held and the information is accurately conveyed.

Training, however, is much, much more, and in many situations the presenting role is one of the least important. Merely considering the five stages in the training cycle indicates that numerous roles are demanded: the skills of needs analysis are very different from those of presenting, the skills of designing a course are very different from those of evaluation, the skills of writing resource material are very different from those of group management, and so on. And many more roles have to be performed, both in the group situation and outside it.

A quick brainstorming of some of the roles required might end up with a surprising checklist:

presenter	person	manager	persuader
psychologist	listener	writer	seller
subject expert	counsellor	innovator	role model
mentor	planner	administrator	technician
agony aunt	leader	organiser	IT adviser
learner	evaluator	motivator	catalyst
coach	creator	diffuser	dogsbody

and many more.

This is an awesome list and none of us can be excellent at all of them. It is more a question of being aware of our strengths, playing to them, and finding ways to combat the weaknesses. We can concentrate on improving on the weaknesses or we can ensure that other people are involved, either from the training team, from members of the group or by requesting external assistance, such as a technician. The important thing is that the event goes well and the learners learn and leave as satisfied customers.

The main role of the trainer is thus that of a *facilitator* – you facilitate by the best method available, using the resources available, the learning and development of the group. While most of this role will be undertaken when the group is actually together, much of it also takes place elsewhere – for example, at the needs analysis stage where one often facilitates the identification of training needs and the release of individuals for training.

Within the training situation most of the roles of the facilitator fall into three distinct categories – subject expert, method expert, and group manager – and these are worthy of further elaboration.

Subject expert

Our delegates expect you to know something about the subject, and the more you know and communicate that knowledge, the more your credibility increases. It is therefore an important part of your own development to update your knowledge of the field.

Our delegates do not expect you to know everything. Nobody can be a complete fountain of knowledge, and if you don't know, admit it – don't flannel. A useful tip here is to recognise any expertise within the group and use it when appropriate. Also, with a very specialised field, consider bringing in an expert for a 'one-off'. Not only does it give expert input of knowledge, it also exposes delegates to a change of style which is often beneficial. One cautionary note: do not create such an aura of expertise that you become unapproachable. Credible experts with the human touch are far more respected. For most people, merely being natural is the best way to achieve this.

Method expert

As will be outlined later in this book, there are numerous learning methods available, and you should be familiar with most and feel comfortable and competent with a few.

Part of your role is to exercise sound, professional judgement on the best method of helping your delegates learn, and sometimes during the event your role can be very low-key.

Becoming competent with a variety of learning methods, including the new forms of IT available, should be a constant goal and should be part of your own professional development. Watch other trainers and learn from them, and risk yourself on occasions and experiment. As in all walks of life, it is only when we risk ourselves that true growth and development occur.

Group manager

This is the area in which the facilitation skills are most obvious. Trainers require a high level of interpersonal skills to be able to manage (not control) a group. The style and role can change from motivator to leader to counsellor, according to the situation.

Trainers must be sensitive to group atmosphere and mood as well as to the individuals present. They need to be able to analyse individuals as well as the group. They need to have some understanding of individual and group psychology, although they do not need to become experts.

Of the three main areas, this is the one where the skills take longest to acquire. Subject competency can be acquired fairly quickly – group facilitation skills take much longer. A good and experienced group facilitator has a skill of enormous power and is able to really harness the synergy within the group to achieve powerful and lasting learning. It is a competency you should strive to acquire, and is best acquired through practice.

The foregoing is a general list to give a broad picture. More detail on many of the roles and how to perform them more competently is included in later chapters.

EXERCISES

1   Consider a trainer you have observed or worked with.
    (a)   What were his/her strengths?
    (b)   What were his/her weaknesses?
    (c)   Why was the trainer successful?
    (d)   Why was the trainer unsuccessful?
    (e)   What did he/she do well?
    (f)   What did he/she do badly?
    (g)   What did you learn from the trainer?
    (h)   If there was a training team, how did the trainers complement each other?

2   Consider three training situations in which you have been involved.
    (a)   For each one, consider the roles played by the trainer(s).
    (b)   How did the trainer(s) help learning?
    (c)   What could have been done better to improve learning?

3   Consider any involvement you have had in the following.
    (a)   Classroom training
    (b)   Outdoor education
    (c)   Training involving sophisticated hardware and software
    (d)   Simulations.

    How effective were each in achieving their objectives? Why?

4   Think of three different trainers you have seen who had different styles. What were those styles? How effective were they?

5   A list of major world changes that have happened in the period 1989–2003 was

given earlier in the chapter. List some of the changes that have taken place in your life in the past five years. What do you need to do to address these changes?

KEY POINTS

The following are the main points with regard to training:

- Training is becoming more widely accepted and recognised as a way of helping individuals and organisations to cope with change and develop.

- Training is a cyclical process with five main stages: analysing, planning and designing, developing, delivering, evaluating.

- There are many types of training available, and learner participation achieves best results.

- Training is not just presenting; it requires a successful execution of a number of roles, both in and out of the classroom.

- The most important role is that of *facilitator* of the learning process. Subject competencies, competence with learning methods and group management skills are essential for success.

FURTHER READING

AMERICAN SOCIETY FOR TRAINING AND DEVELOPMENT (1994) *The Past, Present and Future of Workplace Learning.* Alexandria, Virginia, American Society for Training and Development.

BANK J. (1994) *Outdoor Development for Managers.* 2nd edition. Aldershot, Gower.

BARTRAM S. and GIBSON B. (1997) *Training Needs Analysis.* 2nd edition. Aldershot, Gower.

BUCKLEY R. and CAPLE J. (2000) *The Theory and Practice of Training.* 4th edition. London, Kogan Page.

CHARTERED INSTITUTE OF PERSONNEL AND DEVELOPMENT (2003) 5th Annual Training Survey. London, CIPD.

CONSTABLE J. and McCORMICK R. (1987) *The Making of British Managers.* London, BIM and CBI.

COOPERS and LYBRAND ASSOCIATES (1985) *Challenge to Complacency.* Sheffield, MSC.

COUPLAND D. (1994) *Generation X.* Abacus, London.

HANDY C., GORDON C., GOW I., MALONEY M. and RANDLESOME C. (1987) *The Making of Managers: A report on management education, training and development in USA, West Germany, France, Japan and the UK.* London, NEDO, MSC and BIM.

HACKETT P. (1997) *Introduction To Training.* London, Chartered Institute of Personnel and Development.

PETERSEN R. (1998) *Training Needs Assessment in the Workplace.* 2nd edition. London, Kogan Page.

PONT T. (1995) *Investing in Training and Development: Turning interest into capital.* London, Kogan Page.

PONT T. (1994) 'The role of the management development specialist', in MUMFORD A. (ed.) *Handbook of Management Development.* 4th edition. Aldershot, Gower.

PORTER M. (2003) *UK Competitiveness: Moving to the next stage.* London, Department of Trade and Industry.

RAE L. (1992) *A Guide To In-Company Training Methods.* Aldershot, Gower.

REAY D. (1994) *Identifying Training Needs.* London, Kogan Page.

REID M. A., BARRINGTON H. and KENNEY J. (1999) *Training Interventions: Promoting learning opportunities.* 6th edition. London, Chartered Institute of Personnel and Development.

2 ■ DESIGNING THE COURSE

The designing of a course from nothing can appear a daunting and awesome task, not to mention the time involved. If one adopts a systematic approach, it can greatly help to clarify thinking and create a framework for development.

After reading this chapter, you will be able to:

- describe the main stages in the systematic approach to course design

- spell out some of the main considerations for each of the nine stages in the systematic approach

- use the systematic approach as a framework for the design of future courses.

Many of us have been contacted by someone and asked to take a course. It may vary from a short-duration adult education class at the local centre to a full workshop or programme for senior managers in a famous and exotic international location.

Whatever the location or whatever the level, the role of the trainer is to design a meaningful learning experience for the participants, starting from a blank sheet of paper. At this stage the delivery of the programme seems a million miles away and a multitude of questions begin to emerge, all of which need answering before any design and delivery can begin to take place. Questions that are soon asked and require answering include:

How many delegates are there?
What is their educational level?
What is their seniority?
Why are they coming?
What do they hope to get out of the programme?
Where is it to be held?
What are the facilities?

What visual aids, etc, are available?

What body of knowledge *must* I cover?

       should I cover?

       could I cover?

What *skills* are they hoping to acquire?

To what level of competency?

Why is the organisation sending them?

What are the objectives of the programme? Individual objectives?

            Organisational objectives?

What are the times of the course?

What is the duration of the course?

What methods should I employ?

What resource material shall I need to deliver the programme?

Shall I be on my own?

Will others be helping me?

How shall I know if the course has met its objectives?

These are just a sample of the kinds of question that come into the mind of the trainer in quickfire succession. In order to give clarity of thinking and purpose to this mish-mash of thoughts, it helps to approach the situation in a systematic manner.

The main ideas behind the systematic approach are:

- that as a trainer you should have responsibility for planning the system in which the self-directing needs of your students can be satisfied so that they can learn

- that you have fully analysed and understood the skills and knowledge that your students must develop and the level of competence they should acquire

- that from this analysis you will be able to construct a list of objectives to help you design the course and give you some indication of the resources you will need

- once you have clarified your objectives, that you can devise an appropriate range of learning materials to meet those objectives

- that if you fail to meet your objectives, you must ask why and take the appropriate action to bridge the learning or competency gap.

THE NINE STAGES OF THE SYSTEMATIC APPROACH

Put into a systematic or sequential series of nine stages, these would be the questions you would ask and answer:

1   What is the general aim of the course?

2   What are the key learning objectives?

3   What should be included in the course in terms of knowledge, skills and attitude modification?

4   What are the most appropriate methods of learning to help achieve the objectives?

5   What resources are needed to use these methods?

6   How can the course best be designed to meet the above criteria?

7   What is the best way of presenting/delivering the course?

8   How can the success of the programme be evaluated?

9   How can the programme be refined or improved?

The sequence is shown diagrammatically in Figure 4.

Figure 4 The systematic approach to the development of a course

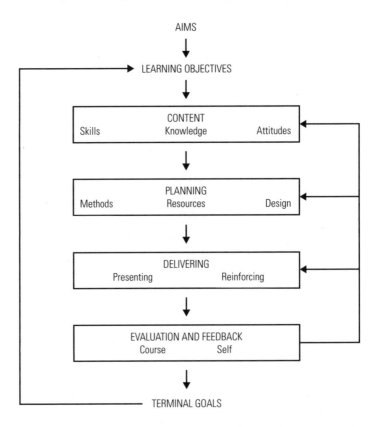

1 Defining the aims

One is often asked, 'What is the difference between an aim and an objective?' In general, an *aim* represents the long-term goals of the course. What do we hope to achieve in broad terms at the end? What goals must the students attain by the end of the programme? Once the overall aims are determined, the trainer can then begin to consider the detailed *objectives* for the course.

2 Defining learning objectives

Learning objectives have also been called performance objectives and behavioural objectives. Whatever the terminology, objectives must be clearly defined.

An objective is a precise goal stated in measurable quantitative or qualitative terms. It is of little use to you in designing a course if vague, woolly terminology is used in defining the objectives.

There are three simple rules to help you define and write down your objectives to enable you to plan your course:

- What can you reasonably expect your students to be able to do, know or think by the end of the course? If you start from the end product or final performance that is expected, it is much easier to plan the first steps.

- Analyse this final performance into the three basic types of learning – knowledge, skills and attitude change. The relative importance of the three types will vary, but they are usually present in differing degrees. All courses have a knowledge (cognitive) content. All teachers are in the business of attitude change (affective learning) – even if only by changing the students' attitudes to a learning process – and the amount of skill acquisition will vary according to the course.

- Be specific in the words you use. It will help you if you avoid vague words like 'knowledge', 'show', 'understand', 'appreciate' and use words like 'list', 'identify', 'use', 'state', 'compare', 'define'.

3 Determining the content

Once the objectives have been decided, it is helpful to draft a course outline of the content needed to provide the delegates with the skills, knowledge and attitudes identified in the objectives. These topics should be arranged in a teaching/learning sequence.

The next stage is to use the objectives and content outline to develop a course of study. The course of study should:

- meet the specific and general objectives of the course

- cover the main topics with supporting detail arranged in a teaching/learning sequence

- contain suggestions on the most effective and efficient ways of presenting the material

- suggest ways in which your delegates' learning can be reinforced by practical experience

- state or consider the range of teaching aids or media needed to present or assist the presentation of material

- consider ways of evaluating the progress of the individual or group against objectives.

It is always helpful to discuss your thoughts or ideas with others, especially those with more experience. This should help you check that you have made no glaring omissions, and can help you crystallise your own thoughts and ideas.

4 Choosing your method

It would be nice and easy to have a grid of all the teaching methods linked to the learning objective so that it would merely be a case of 'reading off' what the appropriate method should be.

Unfortunately, it is not usually as easy as this. There are numerous methods of teaching available, and although it is true that some methods are best suited to certain learning objectives, there is usually some element of choice.

There are, of course, other variables which impact upon the choice of method.

Your students' preferences, abilities and personalities

Recent research, particularly in the area of learning styles, indicates that we all have developed preferred learning habits or styles that help us benefit more from some experiences than from others.

At this point it is not the intention to describe the four styles in detail. Suffice it to say that different personality types with differing levels of intelligence respond differently to, and perhaps get less or more out of, certain situations than others (see Chapter 5).

Your own preferences and abilities

The skills with which to facilitate a learning experience for adults are skills that are acquired over a long period of time. This applies even more when the group members are highly intelligent, are well motivated and occupy senior positions.

Different methods require different skills. Although it would be desirable to be completely at ease with all the great variety of methods, very few attain that overall level of competence. Furthermore, there is little doubt that we all have preferences for working in a certain way. Some love to give a formal lecture and inspire the audience or group with their rhetoric; others prefer to work from within the group in a quiet, self-effacing way.

The best advice that can be offered is:

- As long as the learning objectives and the needs of the student are sure to be met, choose the method with which you feel most comfortable. That is neither being selfish nor neglecting the needs of your students; rather it is allowing you to give of your best for their benefit, and groups usually respond accordingly.

- Bring in someone else who is more competent than you in a certain method. This can be one of the great benefits of team-teaching where two or more facilitators on a programme can compensate for each other's strengths and weaknesses.

The resources available

This would include the accommodation available, audio-visual aids and the amount of help you have. You cannot do small group work if you are alone with 20 participants!

Whatever the influences or considerations, it must be said with regard to method that one should always strive for variety. It exploits the sense of curiosity, enjoyment, excitement, interest and arousal in both trainer and participant alike. In a nutshell, it prevents staleness setting in.

Variety of method is also an important way of catering for the diversity that exists in groups. Even if the educational attainment level is similar, we know that a variety of preferred styles of learning exist. By varying the method we can cater for all preferences within the group and at the same time give everyone the chance to develop other styles of learning, in much the same way that we would exercise and develop a muscle.

5 Determining the resources

In an ideal world a trainer is not bound by a shortage of resources. It is merely a case of deciding upon the ideal programme and obtaining the necessary resources.

Unfortunately, this is rarely the case and the trainer has to consider the resources that are available and tailor the course accordingly. It can happen that, having decided upon the ideal method, the resources are not available. It is therefore advisable to enquire about and consider availability of resources before designing the course.

Resources can be divided into two main categories:

- physical resources
  - location of course
  - size of room and seating
  - audio-visual aids
  - course materials – handouts, case studies, etc

- human resources
  - self
  - colleague(s)
  - course members.

Never underestimate the influence of the course members as a resource. They bring a wealth of experience and can help facilitate the learning of their peers. Also, if the location of the course requires members to travel by motorway, bear in mind that traffic is always heavier on Mondays and Fridays – if possible, avoid these days, or make allowance by starting late on Monday and finishing early on Friday.

6 Designing the course

To date we have identified aims, objectives, content, methods and resources. Now comes the final part of the preparation when we actually put it all together and design the course, section by section. This involves deciding on a plan of action – ie a lesson or session plan. This provides you with the orderly procedures for conducting or facilitating a session efficiently. It should not be long (two pages at the most) but should be complete and practical. It should be written or sectioned in a format that is helpful and meaningful to you, the trainer, and it should give you confidence – not only is it proof that you have prepared adequately, but it is your 'prop' if you need it.

The main points of a session plan include:

- topic

- objectives – the key part

- the time required, and timings

- learning methods

- the audio-visual aids required

- questions for checking and review

- assignment(s) and references.

The importance of planning cannot be overemphasised, however experienced you are. Part of the planning process is mental and part is written. Generally, the more inexperienced we are, the more we tend to feel the need to develop written session plans, which give us confidence and serve as a guide to move the learning along in an orderly fashion.

A series of session plans will constitute your course and are useful because they:

- afford a smooth transition from previous sessions to new material

- ensure sequential and adequate presentation of material

- offer time controls

- provide for the proper use of methods, aids and equipment

- establish a record of material presented and training accomplished

- serve as a guide to the trainer so that important points are not omitted

- help to avoid attempted detours by students and keep you on schedule (if appropriate).

The session plan is your guide and script. It should be flexible to accommodate interruptions, questions and lack of understanding on the part of the learners. Departures from the written plan can be expected as the learners fail to understand some aspect of the work, become interested in a particular part of the session, or contribute to the session from their own experiences. Sometimes a teaching plan may be used over and over again with the occasional minor revision to adjust to changing needs and situations.

There are numerous types of standardised lesson or session plans that can be used. Many trainers have adopted one to suit their own situations.

Below is one session plan form that can be modified according to your own situation.

Topic:
Time and length:
Learning objective(s):
Group/class/target audience:
Student preparation:
Teaching aids required:

Materials for student use:
Handouts required:
Evaluation:
Lesson outline:
- Timing
- Key points
- Delivery sequence
- Briefing for following assignment.

Comments and review to improve

The key to any session plan is the listing of objectives. Always keep these in your mind and consider the behaviour that your learners will be capable of at the end of the session which they were not capable of at the start. This will not only help you focus more clearly, but also help you recognise when the desired changes or results have been accomplished. If you are unsure of what to expect as a result of your session, you are less likely to know if it has happened.

No session plan is perfect, and so always consider ways to improve it. Always review it – and do so soon after the event while it is still fresh in your mind. The session plan is your tool to help you – beforehand to prepare, during the lesson to help conduct a successful learning experience, and afterwards to evaluate whether you have achieved your objectives.

7 Presenting the course

If you have thoroughly prepared, your chances of success are high. Much will be said later in this book about the conducting of the first session, the use of visual aids, techniques of presentation, learning methods, etc, so it will suffice here to give only a broad outline.

Always begin by 'tuning-in' to the group and 'where they are at' – ie what their needs are, and what they already know. Relating the start to their position begins to increase feelings of security and will get initial commitment.

In presenting new information, show how it builds on the existing body of knowledge. The teaching methods you select depend on your personal choice and preferences, the material being presented and the level of students in the group. By choosing an appropriate method, you quickly obtain individual interest and attention so that group management is made easier. From experience, you quickly learn the kind of presentation that is best suited to different situations. This develops your self-confidence, improves your feelings of security and rapport with the group, and shows that your training is producing real learning.

In presenting each session, always err on the side of simplicity. Look for individual interest and expertise, and use it wherever appropriate. Aim for variety during the presentation and use flipcharts, overhead projectors, films, filmstrips, etc if they enhance your message. Allow time for questions and checking that the key points of your presentation have been assimilated. Allow opportunities later in the course for reinforcement of the learning.

Afterwards it may help you to note down the good aspects and areas for improvement in your session. What have *you* learned, and how can your presentation be improved? This is particularly important if you will have to repeat the session at some future date. If you must, rewrite your presentation or session plan.

In the presentation stage you should give the information in orderly steps, working from the simple to the more complex and arranging the presentation in the best possible learning sequence. Remember also: never make your session too long – the quality of learning is not directly related to the length of your session. Once the information has been presented, your learners should have the opportunity to use it, apply it, and work with it as soon as possible. This begins the reinforcement process, introduces variety, and may offer the opportunity to correct misunderstandings, offer additional information and provide individual instruction.

The learning process is now focused on the learner. Your role becomes much more of a facilitator, but you should be readily available to offer help or support. Learners usually enjoy this practical or participative style – they can relate it to themselves and their situation; they can test and apply new concepts or skills; and they can achieve success, which is a great motivator, so they are ready to learn more.

The practical session must be carefully planned to ensure that the task, materials and equipment are available and working for all the participants to use. If it is poorly planned, your own credibility could suffer greatly.

8 Evaluating the course

This step helps to determine the effectiveness of the learning. It is much easier to evaluate knowledge and skills than attitude change. For the knowledge component, written or oral questions may be used. They should test the key points and highlight any individual development points. For the skills component, a performance test may be used – learners carry out a task and are observed and rated.

During the planning stage you will have been aware of items that were included unnecessarily, or of relevant items that were omitted. During the evaluation stage you will become more acutely aware of the need for revision, having piloted the course. Most courses, from inception, need a few deliveries before becoming acceptable, and even then new ideas, methods, etc should be incorporated wherever appropriate.

The main objective of any learning evaluation is for the individuals to realise their progress and their own developmental needs. If they are allowed to realise that themselves, rather than being told, there is greater acceptance and greater commitment to continue learning and to develop. Ownership of their own action plan and commitment to it must surely be the objective of all training courses.

9 Review to improve

This is the final stage of the evaluation, in which we focus on ourselves and look to the future. It involves considering:

- how successful we have been in enabling our learners to achieve their objectives
- how successful we have been as trainers in presenting, in our choice of methods and of visual aids, etc.

In short, how can we improve the course and our performance so that we can do a more professional job? We must learn from analysing our successes and failures and identifying their causes. Feedback here is vital, and we must seek it from our learners and from our colleagues. At times such feedback may be painful, but if we are to learn and develop, then we must seek honest feedback and seek to improve. After all, 'sauce for our learners must be sauce for ourselves'.

AN EXAMPLE OF COURSE DESIGN

The marketing director of a pharmaceutical company is concerned about the high level of staff turnover among medical representatives and the problem of poor performance among some representatives.

The indications are that:

- the level of selection interviewing skills among regional managers is poor
- the regional managers' knowledge of company disciplinary procedure is minimal.

You are asked to design and deliver a two-day course for eight people to improve the regional managers' knowledge of interviewing. This is the aim of the course.

Objectives (remember to look at the final performance) – as a result of attending this course, delegates will be able to:

- list objectives for interviews

- draw up a person specification for a post

- plan and conduct an effective interview for

  - selection purposes

  - disciplinary purposes

- know and be able to use the seven-point plan at a selection interview

- use good questioning techniques

- use good listening techniques

- explain the company disciplinary procedure

- document and assess the evidence and make a recommendation.

Planning

Possible methods to use:

- lectures

- discussions

- case studies

- role-plays

- observation and imitation

- films

- projects.

Possible resources required:

- overhead projector (OHP) and transparencies

- flipcharts, etc

- case study material – best to relate to real-life situations so it comes alive for the participants

- closed-circuit television (CCTV)

- films or videos

- 16mm projector or video recorder

- handouts

- accommodation.

Based upon the foregoing, the design of the two days in broad outline could be:

Day 1		*Method*
9.00	Introductions	
	Expectations	
	Objectives	
	Content and method	
	– selection interviewing	
	– discipline	
	– use of practical exercises	
	(role-plays using CCTV)	
9.45	Interviewing – general principles	Lecture
10.15	Coffee	
10.30	Selection interviewing	
	1 The application form and employee	
	specification	Lecture
	2 Analysing the CV – exercise	Project
	3 The seven-point plan	Lecture
	4 Questioning technique and exercises	Lecture and project
	5 Listening and exercises	Lecture and project
	6 Film	Film
	7 Discussion	Discussion
	8 Review	
12.45	Lunch	
1.45	Practice interviews – using CVs of	
	previous applicants	
	4 × 1-hour interviews	
	– case study and role-play	
	– critique and debrief using peer	
	observation and CCTV	
	NB each case study is different	
	Tea between interviews – approx. 3.45 pm	
5.45	Plenary session – share and compare	
	Learning review	
	Reading assignment	
6.00	Disperse	

Day 2		*Method*
9.00	Issues arising from Day 1	
	Discussion	Discussion
9.15	The company disciplinary procedure	Lecture
	Discussion	Discussion
9.45	The disciplinary interview – stages	Lecture
	Discussion	Discussion
	Film	Film
	Discussion	Discussion
10.30	Coffee	
10.45	Practice interviews	
	2 × 1-hour interviews	
	— case study and role-play	Case study and role-play
	— critique and debrief using peer observation and CCTV	
	— discussion	Discussion
1.15	Lunch	
2.15	Practical disciplinary interviews	
	2 × 1-hour interviews	
	— case study and role-play	Case study and role-play
	— critique and debrief using peer observation and CCTV	
	— discussion	Discussion
	NB each case study is different.	
	Tea between interviews – approx. 3.25 pm	
4.20	Plenary session – share and compare	
	Learning review	
	Disperse	

An example of a draft session plan from this course might look like this:

Course: Interviewing skills for regional managers
Session: Selection interviewing
Time: 10.30 am–1.00 pm

Session outline or element	*Method content, handouts visual aids, etc*
1 The company job application form and specimen employee specification for medical rep. (10.30 am)	■ Lecture/discussion ■ 8 application forms ■ 8 job specifications (10 mins)
2 Analysing the CV – stress the importance of pre-preparation (10.40 am)	■ 8 specimen CVs ■ split into two syndicates, examine CV and compile a list of points to raise at interview (30 mins)
3 The seven-point plan (11.10 am)	■ 8 specimen company assessmentforms ■ brief input to describe plan ■ any questions ■ handout (20 mins)
4 Questioning technique (11.30 am)	■ types of questions – input ■ exercise to spot errors in questioning – 8 handouts ■ do exercise in pairs ■ share in plenary handout (25 mins)
5 Listening (11.55 am)	■ input about techniques of summarising ■ in pairs, exercise to practise it ■ input on technique of reflecting ■ in pairs, exercise to practise it ■ discussion ■ give out handouts (25 mins)

6 Film (12.20 pm)	■ video
	■ show *Manhunt*
	■ discussion
	■ relate to earlier parts
	of a session
	(35 mins)
7 Review of morning (12.55 pm)	discussion
	(5 mins)

The level of detail required is a matter for individual choice. Inexperienced trainers will probably need to go into greater detail than experienced trainers. The important part to stress is that your preparation should enable you to do a good job, and you should therefore plan the session to a level of detail that satisfies your comfort level and boosts your confidence.

EXERCISES

1 Consider a course you have been involved in designing.
   (a) How did you go about it?
   (b) What went well? Why?
   (c) What went badly? Why?
   (d) What would you repeat next time?
   (e) What would you do differently?

2 If you have to design a new course in the near future, you might like to use the nine stages in the systematic approach as a guide. Once you become familiar with it, and with using it, you will find it a useful tool in all future design work. Remember: practice makes perfect.

KEY POINTS

In order to deliver a course successfully, the main requirements are:

- Determine and understand the broad aim.

- Establish objectives (stated in terms of future learner accomplishments).

- Plan thoroughly beforehand
  - determine the content
  - choose your method(s) and strive for variety
  - be aware of available resources and assemble them
  - develop individual session plans.

- Maintain competence in delivering the training
  - put delegates at ease and always relate to their needs
  - present slowly and clearly
  - check for understanding
  - involve the participants.

- Allow ample opportunities for reinforcement.

- Evaluate thoroughly
  - participants' learning
  - self.

FURTHER READING

HARDINGHAM A. (1996) *Designing Training.* London, Chartered Institute of Personnel and Development.

LEATHERMAN D. (1996) *Designing Training Programmes.* Aldershot, Gower.

RAE L. (1997) *Planning and Designing Training Programmes.* Aldershot, Gower.

STIMSON N. (2002) *How to Write and Prepare Training Materials.* 2nd edition. London, Kogan Page.

3 ■ DELIVERING THE COURSE – THE START-UP

The early part of any course is the most crucial. The design and content of a course may be first-class, but that is no guarantee that all will go well. Much can be done behind the scenes to increase your chances of success.

After reading this chapter, you will:

- be familiar with many of the key tasks that have to be performed beforehand in preparation for the course

- appreciate the benefits of some of the main forms of room layout

- be aware of some of the things that you can do to prepare yourself

- be able to select and use a method of getting the first session under way.

The course has been designed and all the preparation associated with it has been completed. You are ready to deliver. Considerable thought must be put towards the first session to ensure its success, and there is every reason to give yourself the best possible chances of achieving it. Although you may have a good command of the subject content and be equally familiar with the teaching methodology, that alone is no guarantee of success. The first session is the most crucial of the whole course. It is the time for weighing up – when the first impressions are made that are so vitally important. In any interactive situation it is so much easier at a later stage if you set off on the right track – it is easier to stay on track than get back on it. It is therefore vital that you give more attention and thought to the start-up than to any other part of the course.

The first session usually sets the tone for the rest of the course. What can we do to improve our chances of (a) making a good first impression, and (b) being successful?

PREPARATION FOR THE COURSE

Before start-up

For the inexperienced trainer the time spent on this phase is much greater than for the experienced trainer. As a general rule of thumb, the inexperienced trainer probably needs to spend at least three hours' preparation for every hour's presentation. Although the ratio of preparation time to presentation time may diminish for the experienced trainer, preparation should still be carried out. Complacency is a bigger threat than inexperience, and delegates are less tolerant of this than inexperience.

If advice can be given on preparation, err on the side of over-preparation rather than under-preparation. The belief that 'It will be all right on the night' tends to hold true only if you have done your homework.

To help you ensure that all the details have been taken care of, it is useful to prepare a 'trainer checklist'. Not only will this help you to ensure that everything has been carried out first time round, but it will make life easier on subsequent occasions and, perhaps, for your successor. It is also something that can be altered in the light of experience. A simple checklist is outlined below.

Course/lesson	
Date	
Location	
Number of delegates	
Number of rooms	
Trainer(s)	

Item/task	Required	Done	Comments
Joining instructions (a) map (b) delegate list (c) course outline (d) transport arrangements			
Meals (a) times (b) menus (c) coffee breaks			
Recreation (a) times (b facilities			
Accommodation reservations (a) delegates (b) trainer(s) (c) guest speaker(s)			
Training materials (a) handouts (b) exercise materials (c) films, videos, etc			

Visual aids
 (a) screen
 (b) film projector(s)
 (c) OHP (and spare bulb)
 (d) demonstration or practice equipment
 (e) flipcharts/whiteboards
  (i) pads
  (ii) easel
  (iii) pens (water-based for a whiteboard)
  (iv) Blu-Tack or masking tape
  (v) other AV devices
  (vi) extension cables
  (vii) whiteboard eraser			

Item/task	Required	Done	Comments
Training room (a) layout (b) refreshments (c) fire exit procedures			

Materials for delegates
(a) advance materials, eg
       reading
(b) name tags
(c) joining instructions (eg
       pre-course questionnaires
       or exercises)
(d) pencils
(e) paper
(f) books
(g) hole punch
(h) folders
(i) clipboards
(j) course certificate
(k) course mementos, eg
       photos, gifts, etc			

Trainer materials (a) handouts (b) lesson plan (c) visuals (d) mastercopies (e) (own materials)			
Course evaluation forms			
Others			

Preparing the physical learning environment

Much of the training will take place in purpose-built accommodation, but some will also take place in rooms that were never designed with training in mind. Whatever the situation, a lot can be done to ensure that the physical environment assists rather than impedes learning – and the trainer can do much to affect the physical environment.

Wherever possible I would always advocate a visit to the learning environment *before* a course. This is even more important if the venue is unfamiliar to you because you may have the opportunity to change a poor location, either within the building or elsewhere. Even if you are using a very familiar setting and those who normally pre-prepare the room are reliable, you must still check beforehand that everything is to your satisfaction. The ultimate responsibility for ensuring that everything is satisfactory rests with the trainer.

Things you can check with regard to training rooms include:

■ Visit the room beforehand and assess suitability for the event.

■ Check that the size is right – not too small or too large. Does it have adjoining syndicate rooms that are appropriate?

■ Ensure that the room is designed and furnished appropriately. For example, I recently made a visit to a new hotel to inspect a training room only to discover a simulated marble floor without carpets which gave a cold and austere atmosphere.

■ Ensure that there is adequate ventilation, light and heating.

■ Ensure that there are adequate toilet and washing facilities.

■ Check that the environment 'feels good' and has an atmosphere conducive to interaction and learning.

Room layout

Much can be done with the furniture of a room to achieve the objectives of the course. The layout should maximise learner comfort and serve a purpose. If the learners are using equipment such as PCs, they will need a table and chair and room to lay out their worksheets, texts, instructions, etc. If, on the other hand, the group is involved in little note-taking and a variety of experiential activities, tables and chairs may get in the way and so a circle of chairs may be a much more effective arrangement. (Figures 5 to 12 show examples of seating plans.)

Figure 5 Horseshoe

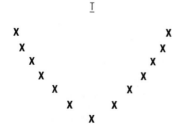

Suitable for small numbers, up to 20 learners

■ Good for experiential activities.
■ Promotes discussion, interaction and sense of identity.
■ Informal and allows tutor to be very close to the group.
■ Facilitates use of visual aids.

Figure 6 Table layout

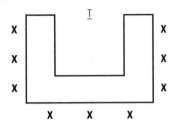

Ideal for groups of less than 20.

- Gives learners plenty of space.
- Allows tutor to move freely within the group.
- Facilitates use of visual aids.
- Promotes discussion.
- Allows delegates to do individual work.

Figure 7 Boardroom shape

This offers similar advantages to the previous layout, but does not allow the tutor to move as freely within the group.

Figure 8 Classroom shape

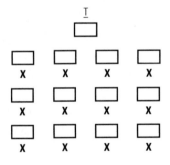

This is one way of accommodating large numbers.

- Evokes feelings of being 'back at school'.
- Does not encourage interaction and participation.

Figure 9 Theatre shape (1)

T

X X X X X X

X X X X X X

X X X X X X

This arrangement is good for formal presentations, especially to large audiences.

- Visual aids easy to use.
- Does not encourage interaction and participation.
- Sets speaker apart, which may threaten speaker, who may then give below-par performance.

Figure 10 Theatre shape (2)

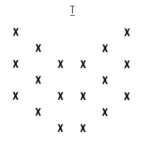

The benefits and disadvantages of this arrangement are similar to those of Figure 9.

Figure 11 Group

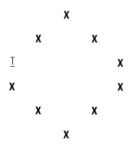

Suitable for small numbers, probably up to 12

- Intimate in that it makes the tutor part of the group.
- Informal and an excellent way to promote discussion.
- Can be difficult to use OHP and other visual aids.

Figure 12 Working conference

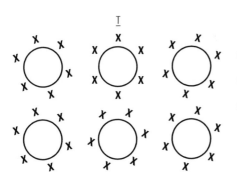

Suitable for large numbers.

- Allows group work to take place during conference and after presentation.
- Groups can become inattentive and talk during presentation.
- Those with backs to the speaker must turn round for speaker's presentation.

Trainer's layout

You must give yourself a place with plenty of space in which to do the tutoring or facilitating. Figure 13 is a diagram of how a room should be arranged for about 12 people.

Figure 13 Suggested layout for a training room

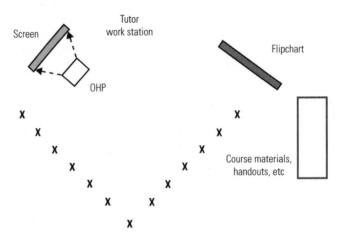

Notice how much room the tutor needs for the OHP, flipchart(s), spare pens/bulbs and handouts. Give a lot of thought beforehand to how you like to work and what makes you feel comfortable. Do you like to stand or sit? Do you prefer/need to have a small table at the front? Can the delegates clearly see what you are presenting? Is your equipment correctly positioned?

Such an arrangement takes a great deal of time and should be made long before the course starts. You must never assume that the room will be ideally suited to your needs. It is the trainer's responsibility to have the training room furniture appropriately arranged, the course materials in order, the projectors working and focused, and an adequate supply of flipchart paper and pens.

Always allow plenty of time to set out the room as you want it before the delegates arrive.

Other considerations

Trainer's toolkit

This usually consists of two main items:

- your own 'masters', or folder of resource material – this material is for use when you decide to digress from the printed programme or when the material you expected to be present has not materialised! In either case, with the assistance of the photocopying facility at the hotel or conference centre, you can manage the situation

- a basic box or bag of items or things you may need at short notice, such as:
    - a pack of file paper
    - Sellotape
    - Blu-Tack
    - a stapler
    - rubber bands
    - correction fluid
    - plain file cards
    - OHP extending pointer
    - paper clips
    - hole punches, two- and four-hole
    - scissors
    - artist's knife or scalpel
    - pencils
    - Post-it pads
    - a glue stick
    - a small screwdriver
    - spare flipchart pens – various colours
    - OHP pens and loose acetates
    - methylated spirits and tissues (for cleaning acetates and OHP lenses!)
    - an electric extension cable
    - video cassette tapes
    - self-adhesive name tags
    - a ruler

You would be amazed how often such items can be of use on a training course.

Catering arrangements and breaks

Meals and break times form an important part of any course. They can add considerably to the enjoyment and success of the course. Conversely, they can be an inflexible barrier which interferes with the smooth operation of a course and the delegates' learning.

It is important that your requirements are understood by the host establishment and that your group is fully aware of what the arrangements are.

It is advisable to take your coffee, tea and meal breaks outside the conference room so that people have an opportunity to get out. For some it may be their only opportunity to smoke if a no-smoking rule has been applied by the group. It also offers the opportunity for informal interaction with and between course members and helps establish more positive relationships. Breaks may also give you the opportunity to deal with any problems that have arisen, sometimes behind the scenes, so that your own credibility does not suffer.

As for lunch, it is best to try to arrange a light lunch, again out of the conference room, and of the self-service variety. A heavy lunch does nothing to prevent drowsiness during the post-lunch session (often called 'the graveyard session') while a lunch reliant upon waiter service can result in lengthy delays, delegate frustration and a late return to the course. Furthermore, if the business of eating is over relatively quickly, delegates have the opportunity to walk in the fresh air, or to do something else to relax their minds and make them more ready for the afternoon session.

With regard to the post-lunch session, as a general rule it is often best to make it a practical one rather than a theoretical one, and to ensure that the interval between lunch and afternoon tea is not too long. Anything that gets delegates into the participative mode after lunch is usually welcomed.

It is also worth stating here that there is no direct relationship between the amount and quality of learning and the time spent in formal sessions. Most people are all too aware of the high costs of mounting and running a training event and therefore strive to maximise the use of time. Trainers sometimes therefore fall into the trap of running formal sessions until very late in the evening. It is important to give delegates some time to relax and also time to discuss items informally. Many groups have spent long hours in the bar in the evening discussing work or course-related issues, but at their choice and beyond the confines of formal sessions.

The option of a mid-course break on long residential courses should be given. A change of activity or a short opportunity to escape the confines of the host establishment can be very welcome and energising. Equally, delegates usually respond to and welcome the opportunity of an early departure on the last day to beat the traffic and get home.

Messages and interruptions

Arrangements must be made beforehand for the collection of messages. It is important that sessions are not interrupted and that people receive messages during break times. Ensure that delegates know the system for the receipt of messages.

It is suggested that contracts are made by course members with regard to contact with work. This is especially important with in-house courses where the temptation to check the in-tray is much stronger. As far as possible, try to persuade people to become 'unavailable' for the duration of the course. And you must abide by the same rules yourself.

PREPARING YOURSELF

All the necessary administrative arrangements have been completed and you have given yourself the best possible chance of success in designing the physical learning environment and ensuring that all the administrative arrangements have been made.

If these have been correctly implemented, you have considerably increased your chances of success. There are other things that you can do and can control to increase the chances of success even further:

Be smart, clean and well-groomed. This gives a professional appearance. Your image and attire contribute to the atmosphere. There are no hard-and-fast rules on what to wear. Generally, in-house courses have a more formal attire.

At conference centres and hotels more casual dress is often the rule.

It is important to 'tune in' to the dress code of the organisation for which you are providing the training and make the appropriate adjustments. You usually find, certainly off-site, that standards become more relaxed once you get under way.

It is always advisable to take some formal clothes with you, particularly if there is likely to be a formal dinner during the training event, perhaps with visiting dignitaries. You may not need such attire, but if you have it, you have more options.

Strive for a comfortable, relaxed, friendly but positive environment. Some ways in which you can do this are to:

- welcome people
- smile
- be enthusiastic.

Be conscious of your body language and that of others. Maintain good eye contact. Smile. Keep up a good, open posture. Avoid distracting mannerisms. More will be said about this later in the book.

Establish your credibility and that of your colleague(s). Never apologise for being there and thereby demean yourself. Equally, do not build up such an aura of expertise that you become unapproachable.

Relax. Be yourself. If you appear tense or over-anxious, that will transfer itself to others. Thorough preparation beforehand should give you confidence. In addition you can:

- take a few moments before the event to relax and gather your thoughts
- breathe deeply and slowly in a short, private session on your own

- talk to your colleague, particularly if he or she is much more experienced – and if you need support, ask for it since counselling and supporting each other during the training event is a very therapeutic activity and a good confidence-booster

- observe old pros doing their act and copy their good habits, if appropriate. This can be one great benefit of the team-teaching approach.

You may also wish to do regular relaxation exercises at suitable points during a course. There is a variety of books and tapes available on this subject. Try some exercises, and if they work for you, go on using them.

Be careful with your time-keeping. As part of presenting a professional image it is important that prompt starts are made and that the group understands this. If you are prompt and punctual, the group will be the same. If you are late and sloppy, the group will follow that trend.

More flexibility should be allowed with regard to finishing times. If the group is engaged in meaningful activity and learning, then let it continue. Equally, if it appears that nothing positive is to be gained by prolonging a session to the stated time, finish early or give the delegates a leisure or private study option. There is nothing worse than keeping tired and disinterested delegates chained to their seats at the end of the day for a meaningless activity and frustrating them even more.

Rules relating to time-keeping are established at the start of the course as part of your contract with the group. If you ensure that you keep to the contract, your credibility will be enhanced.

THE FIRST MEETING – GETTING ACQUAINTED

Whatever the level of course or whatever the level of the participants, each course is a new experience. An element of the unknown exists for everybody, tutor included.

We have looked elsewhere at the impact of the environment upon the learning process and stressed the importance of the appropriate arrangement of furniture so that interaction between tutor and delegates and between delegates themselves can take place freely.

Another important part of the environment is what we can loosely term 'climate'. It is a difficult concept to define, but a positive or negative climate can have an enormous impact upon the learning process.

A climate that is characterised by tenseness, low trust, formality, coldness or aloofness, or that is authority-oriented, competitive and judgemental, is *not* conducive to learning.

A climate that is characterised by a relaxed atmosphere, mutual trust and respect, informality, warmth, collaboration and mutual support *is* conducive to learning.

In a nutshell, if participants feel good about themselves and the experience, and if they feel secure and their levels of anxiety are low, you are well on the way to achieving a positive outcome.

The establishment of such a positive climate is not achieved immediately. One cannot just press a button, as if turning on the lights, in order to create the right climate. It needs work, and it starts at the beginning of a course.

In fact, for both tutor and delegates the first meeting or first session is the most crucial. It is the time of getting to know one another, forming impressions and deciding whether to make a commitment. One of the main objectives, if not *the* main objective, of the first session is to begin the process of getting acquainted so that levels of anxiety can be reduced. It is the first step in the process of climate-setting, and it is as much for the benefit of the tutor as it is for the delegate.

Many years ago, when I took up my first teaching post in a secondary school, an old hand took me aside and gave me a little fatherly advice. 'You have to have discipline,' he said. 'Until you have got them under control you can't teach them anything.'

In respect of an adult situation, the advice could be 'You have to have them feeling secure and relatively free from anxiety – otherwise, they will not be in a position to learn.'

Having stated *what* we should do, we then have again to ask *how we* should do it. How should we begin the process of establishing a positive climate and of allaying people's anxieties, including our own? In other words, how should we break the ice?

It is important to devote the first session to breaking the ice and commencing the getting-acquainted process (unless, of course, everyone already knows everyone else, which is rare).

A number of icebreaking exercises are now available. It is important to choose one, or to devise your own, that is appropriate to the group. A common method that I have used many times is the Pairs Interviews icebreaker, sometimes referred to as 'Jack and Jill'. A version of this is reproduced below and can be adapted in several ways.

Pairs Interviews icebreaker ('Jack and Jill')

Activity outline

This exercise asks the delegates, working in pairs, to informally interview each other and then to introduce their partner to the rest of the group. It is an exercise that is generally more effective if carried out at the start of a course after the tutors have introduced themselves.

Training application

Time allowed: approx. 5 to 10 minutes for each interview.

Group size: best suited to groups of 8 to 16 participants.

Space required: a large conference area in which delegates can move their chairs to guarantee some privacy. If adjoining syndicate rooms are available, they should be used.

Materials needed: none.

Trainer administration

1   The trainer begins by explaining the need to get to know one another – that because delegates usually feel more embarrassed talking about themselves than about others, each delegate will introduce one other person to the group.

2   Delegates are asked to pair off, and if possible choose someone they do not know. (If they are hesitant, the trainer can randomly decide the pairing. Should it be necessary, one group may contain three members.)

3   Each pair is to find a place in which to work with some degree of privacy. The pair is then to spend 5–10 minutes interviewing each other, learning each other's names and sharing information about background, interests, values, goals, etc.

4   The group leader may wish to call out the time when one minute remains so that both partners have an opportunity to share information about themselves.

5   When the allotted time has elapsed, the trainer calls the whole group together.

6   When the group has assembled, the trainer explains that each person will introduce his or her partner to the group. Each person is allowed two minutes for the introduction. For example: 'This is Jill. She is a pharmacist and lives here in town. She was born in Edinburgh and graduated at …', and so on.

7   The trainer asks for a pair to volunteer to begin the introductions. The exercise continues until all the group members have been introduced.

Variations

■   Delegates talk to the group as if they were their partners. For example: 'My name is Jill …' Or they stand behind their partner's chair for the introduction.

■   If the members of a group appear to be uninhibited, the group leader can ask the partners to perform the introductions by acting out each other's key characteristics or personal traits.

■ The trainer can encourage the group members to ask questions about the person who is being introduced. The partner must answer the questions to the best of his or her ability. Then the person being introduced responds as to the accuracy of his or her partner's statements.

Note: The variations are numerous, each one requiring a degree of risk-taking on the part of the delegate. It is the role of the trainer to sense what is appropriate for the group in question.

EXERCISES

1   Consider three different training events in which you have been involved.
    (a)   Describe the physical learning environment.
    (b)   How did it contribute to the success of the course?
    (c)   How did it detract from the success of the course?

2   List some of your feelings in different group situations where the layout was different.
    (a)   What have you learned about yourself?
    (b)   What can you do in the role of trainer to improve your comfort level?

3   Consider an experienced trainer you have observed.
    (a)   How did he or she arrange the environment and use it to enhance learning?
    (b)   What did you learn, and what could you adopt?

4   How do you feel before a training event? What, if anything, do you do beforehand to combat any anxieties? What has a positive effect? What else could you do to make yourself more relaxed?

5   List three different icebreakers you have observed.
    (a)   Were they successful?
    (b)   What were the benefits for yourself (if in the training role) and for the participants?
    (c)   List anything you learned from your observations.

KEY POINTS

Major points from this chapter include:

- Detailed planning and preparation beforehand increases the chances of success.

- The physical learning environment can have a profound effect upon learning, and considerable thought and attention should be given to the layout.

- The first session is crucial – 'icebreakers' help greatly in getting people interacting and launching the course in a positive way.

FURTHER READING

BARCA M. and COBB K. (1993) *Icebreakers 2: Beginnings and Endings*. Aldershot, Gower.

BARTRAM S. and GIBSON B. (1994) *Activities for Developing Training Skills*. Aldershot, Gower.

HART L. B. (1996) *Icebreakers 3: Icebreakers, Links and Energisers*. Aldershot, Gower.

JONES K. (1995) *Icebreakers. A Source of Games, Exercises, and Simulations*. 2nd edition. Aldershot, Gower.

KIRBY A. (1992) *Games for Trainers* (Vols 1 and 2). Aldershot, Gower.

KIRBY A. (1993) *Icebreakers 1*. Aldershot, Gower.

KIRBY A. (1994) *Games for Trainers* (Vol. 3). Aldershot, Gower.

NEWSTON J. W. and SCANNEL E. (1980) *Games Trainers Play: Experiential learning exercises*. San Francisco, McGraw-Hill.

ORRIDGE M. (1998) *How To Deliver Training*. Aldershot, Gower.

SIDDONS S. (1997) *Delivering Training*. London, Chartered Institute of Personnel and Development.

UNIVERSITY ASSOCIATES (1983) *Encyclopaedia of Icebreakers*. Tucson, Arizona, University Associates.

4 ■ LEARNING THEORY

It is important that trainers have some knowledge and understanding of the learning process, particularly in the case of an adult. This will help you immensely in both the design and the delivery of a course.

After reading this chapter, you will:

■ be able to describe the process of learning and define its three component parts

■ know the difference between traditional teaching and learner-directed training

■ distinguish between product and process

■ be familiar with some of the main groups of learning theory and how they might be applied in training

■ know all about the four stages of the learning cycle

■ be aware of the four major learning styles.

Learning theory has evolved over the past century as a result of numerous experiments that have been conducted, often with animals. Different schools of psychological thinking have made their various contributions to our pool of knowledge. No single theory has obtained complete agreement among psychologists about the details of the learning process, but they all accept the basic premiss that learning occurs whenever one adopts new, or modifies existing, behaviour patterns in a way that has some influence on future performance or attitudes.

Learning is not about behaviour changes that occur as a result of the maturation process, but is about a change in behaviour that is reasonably permanent and must grow out of past experience. It follows, therefore, in the case of an adult whose reservoir of experience is so much greater, that any behaviour change must occur as a result of a deeper and more meaningful experience than that of a child. Some of the theories of learning that have been applied to the teaching of children may thus not be as effective if applied to the teaching of adults. The adult learner is a species that is somewhat different from the child learner, and this should be reflected in the design, method and delivery of a training event.

Harris and Schwann reiterate that 'Learning is essentially change due to experience', but then go on to distinguish between learning as a product (which explains the end result or outcome of the learning experience), learning as a process (which emphasises what happens during the course of learning experience in attaining a given learning product or outcome) and learning as a function (which emphasises certain critical aspects of learning, such as motivation, retention and transfer) that all together make behavioural changes through human learning possible.

Early learning theories fall into two major categories:

- Behaviourist or stimulus-response theories – These include the diverse theories of Thorndike, Pavlov, Skinner and Hull
- cognitive theories – These include those of Tolman and the Gestalt psychologists. They tend to deal more with the acquisition of knowledge.

Types of learning can be categorised into three groups:

- cognitive learning
- psychomotor learning
- affective learning.

Cognitive learning

This means knowledge learning. It includes not only the knowledge *per se*, but also what to do with it or how to apply it. The investigative process and the principles of problem-solving and decision-making are thus part of this group.

Much learning of this nature is imparted by the lecture method, but can be reinforced by a variety of methods such as private study, process reviews, role-plays and case studies.

Psychomotor learning

Psychomotor skills are the physiological skills that are required in order to complete a task. Examples would be those used in driving a car or giving an oral presentation.

The most effective environment in which to gain these physical skills is the 'laboratory', in which students actually gain hands-on experience. The lecturer only prepares the students by giving them the knowledge before entering the arena to practise. It is only in the arena that the real learning takes place. This experiential approach is used, for example, in the training of airline pilots in simulators.

In no area of learning is the old Chinese proverb more appropriate:

I hear, I forget.
I see, I remember.
I do, I understand.

Affective learning

This is related to attitudes, values and interests, and is the most difficult training of all, mainly because it is tricky to measure.

Such changes tend to occur as a result of the training process. They can certainly be influenced by such factors as trainer style, facilitation skills, the learning environment and the learning method. Some of the techniques used in management development or team-building programmes that involve the use of CCTV and psychometric inventories can be very powerful in effecting attitudinal change. Such techniques, however, need a high level of sensitivity and facilitation skills, particularly on the part of the trainer, if they are to have a positive effect. Unskilfully and unprofessionally handled, more harm than good can result.

GROUPS OF LEARNING THEORY

There is no one unified theory of adult learning. Over the past century there have evolved many theories of learning, and a comprehensive overview of all these theories would constitute a book in its own right. Such a detailed review of them all is clearly beyond the scope of this book, but for those who wish to study them in more detail, the *Further Reading* section at the end of this chapter will serve as a good starting point.

There is no one theory which is the best or has more to recommend it than the others. Learning is a complex process and each theory can have a practical application some of the time. Depending upon your objectives, one theory or group of theories may be more relevant to the design of your training event, and influence your methodology. The intention of this chapter is therefore to give a brief outline of a number of learning theories that may be relevant. These include one or two new developments in the field. The intention is, then, not to offer a sound, academic classification of learning theories but to heighten the reader's awareness of their existence and their possible implications for training.

The following main groups of learning theories are outlined:

- reinforcement (or stimulus-response) theories
- cognitive theories
- a process model of adult learning
- experiential learning
- learning to learn and self-development
- mental processes
- emerging horizons.

Reinforcement (or stimulus-response) theories

The most famous exponents of this set of theories are Pavlov and Skinner, who carried out numerous experiments with animals. A basic premiss of the theories is that individuals' behaviour can be *conditioned*, and a key element in this process is *reinforcement*. Pavlov is associated with *classical conditioning* following experimentation with dogs, and Skinner is associated with *operant conditioning* following experimentation with rats and pigeons. The Skinnerian term is derived from the fact that the individual must act or operate on the environment in order to be rewarded (operant behaviour).

Most of Pavlov's work (*circa* 1880) was limited to physiological reflex actions, particularly the salivation reflex in dogs. By accident he discovered that dogs would salivate when a previously unconnected stimulus, besides food, was present, provided that on a number of previous occasions the stimulus appeared at or just before the presentation of the food. As a result of this, Pavlov was able to teach dogs to associate salivation with an unconnected stimulus – in the case of the experiments conducted, the sound of a tuning-fork. By pairing the sound of a tuning-fork with the presentation of meat, the dog could be conditioned, as a result of association, to salivate at the sound of the tuning-fork. This is the process of classical conditioning and has limited practical application in the training situation.

Skinner (*circa* 1935) placed hungry rats in boxes containing levers which, when pressed, caused the release of food pellets. Exploratory behaviour by the rats occasionally resulted in a chance contact with a lever. After several accidental lever contacts the rat realised the relationship between pressing the lever and obtaining food. This is trial-and-error learning in which the rat rewards or reinforces its own behaviour.

When the rat obtained the food pellet every time it pressed the lever, Skinner called it *continuous reinforcement*. When the rat was rewarded only occasionally, he called it *intermittent reinforcement*. In the early stages of conditioning, continuous reinforcement is needed to establish the stimulus-response (S-R) link. When the rat is no longer hungry, its perseverance wanes and intermittent reinforcement can be introduced, involving gradually increasing intervals between each reward.

By using varying schedules of intermittent and continuous reinforcement with food pellets, Skinner taught a pigeon to walk in a figure of eight. Over a short period of time the appropriate movement in either a clockwise or anti-clockwise direction was suitably rewarded.

A modern day and commercial application of operant conditioning can be witnessed in the Sea World amusement parks of California and Florida. One example is an act in which Shamu, a large killer whale, jumps out of the water to clear a rope – a feat which brings gasps of admiration from large audiences who also ponder 'How do they do that?' The answer is by operant conditioning, in which good or desirable behaviour by the killer whale is reinforced by the reward of a fish. In the early days of training (or conditioning) a rope is placed under the surface of the water. Every time the whale swims under the rope no reward is offered; every time the whale swims above the rope it is rewarded with a fish. Once the whale has established the connection between the desired behaviour (swimming above the rope) and the reward (a fish), the rope is gradually raised until it is clear of the water. If the whale wants a fish it has to jump clear of the water. From such experiments several valuable conclusions about learning and motivation can be drawn:

- Each step in the learning process should be short and grow out of previously learned behaviour.

- In the early stages, learning should be regularly rewarded and all stages carefully controlled by a schedule of continuous and/or intermittent reinforcement.

- Reward should quickly follow the correct response. This is called *feedback* and is based on the principle that motivation is enhanced when we are informed of our progress. It is linked to the first conclusion above because in order to ensure a high success rate, the steps in the learning process must be small and within the capabilities of the learner.

Operant conditioning has important lessons for both parents and managers in their day-to-day dealings with offspring and subordinates, respectively. It also underpins the design of programmed learning and more recent, sophisticated developments in computer-based learning. By receiving positive feedback, learners are encouraged to continue and extend their learning.

Cognitive theories

Many psychologists believe that human behaviour is too complex for simple S-R theories to offer a rational explanation. They believe that something happens internally between stimulus and response, possibly through information processing, and this would explain behaviour. Among the things that might happen are 'understanding', 'thinking', 'reflection', 'analysis of experience', 'memorising', 'retrieving' or 'remembering'. All of these enable the individual to experience *insight,* which is a key concept of *Gestalt* psychology or cognitive theory. Insight occurs when a solution to a problem becomes obvious and is a solution which can be used again in a similar situation or new situations.

The first demonstration of insightful learning was made by Kohler who, in the Canary Islands in the 1920s, experimented with chimpanzees. Bananas were placed at varying distances, out of reach, outside the chimpanzees' cage. A number of short, individual sticks inside the cage could, if slotted together, be used to reach and procure the bananas. Kohler observed that after a period of unproductive exploratory activity, 'the penny dropped' (insight) and the chimpanzees could solve the problem. Further experiments in which bananas were hung from the roof of the cage and individual boxes were strewn around the cage floor produced similar results.

The emphasis, therefore, in Gestalt psychology is on the adaptability in the use of existing knowledge to form new insights rather than programmed repetition of stimulus-response pairings. It is concerned with the internal processes that we use to recognise and define problems and seek solutions. Solutions can be reached either by trial and error, by deduction, by seeking information and assistance, or by a combination of all three. We see the situation as a whole and begin to make sense of it and recognise it. It is therefore more likely that solutions can be more easily reached by working in groups rather than as solitary individuals – as was the case with Kohler's chimpanzees. Once the methodology and solution(s) have been internalised, transfer of learning to future situations should occur.

Cognitive theories have been applied in a training situation to the technique of discovery learning and problem-solving, which have equal application for child and adult learners. With this technique the trainee, upon being give a task, has to search and sift clues on how best to progress. A means of unassisted learning through experience is provided that will hopefully lead to the development of insights into key relationships and solutions.

From the trainer's point of view, the design of the task is crucial. On training courses, a number of structured experiences (carefully designed tasks intended to produce a specific outcome and therefore learning) can be used. In developing new ones it is essential that they are piloted several times to ensure that they achieve their objectives.

A process model of adult learning

It was only after the Second World War that serious enquiry really began into adult learning and development. Most of this early research took place in the USA.

At the same time in Europe the concept of a unified theory of adult learning had been evolving for which the term *andragogy* was used to differentiate it from the theory of youth learning, *pedagogy*. This term was used by Malcolm Knowles in his work of developing a unified system of adult learning. It is essentially a process model and is based around the premiss that as individuals mature, their need and capacity to be self-directing, to utilise their experience in learning, to identify their own readiness to learn, and to organise their learning around life problems, increases steadily from infancy to pre-adolescence and then increases rapidly during adolescence.

If the culture of the institution or social system, such as a school or family unit, denies or negates the need and ability to be self-directing, the result is tension, resistance, resentment and even rebellion in the individual. Motivational theorists need look no further for many of the problems that exist today in our schools and colleges.

Andragogical theory is based on the following four assumptions that distinguish it from pedagogy or traditional teaching methods:

- the concept of the learner
- the role of learner's experience
- readiness to learn
- orientation to learning.

A more detailed comparison of the two approaches with regard to the four different assumptions is given in Table 1.

Implications for the trainer

1   Motivation of individuals is an intrinsic process (the 'push from within', which is self-generated), so that they are self-directing. The role of the trainer is to create a learning environment that harnesses these intrinsic drives, and not an environment that suppresses them. An informal environment is best. Formality can create tension, and tension impedes learning.

Table 1 Pedagogy *v* Andragogy

With regard to	Pedagogy	Andragogy
Concept of the learner	Role of learner is dependent Teacher takes responsibility for the whole learning process	Role of learner is essentially self-directing Role of teacher is to encourage and nurture this self-directed need
Role of learners' experience	Learners bring little experience to the learning situation Learners dependent on 'expert' input Main techniques are transmittal techniques	Learners' experience accumulated over a lifetime is a great resource for learning both for self and others Learners attach greater significance to what they experience than to what they are told Main techniques are experiential techniques
Readiness to learn	Learners learn what they are conditioned to learn to obtain parental, societal approval Fear of failure is a great motivator Learning is standardised and progressive because it is aimed at the same age group, and every age group is similar in its learning needs and its	Learners learn when they feel a need to learn Learning should meet their needs to cope with the demands of their world – home, work, etc Learning should be organised to meet learner needs and sequenced according to the individual's ability and readiness to learn
Orientation to learning	Learning is subject-oriented, with emphasis on content, most of which they may forget because it has no immediate relevance (principle of 'deferred gratification')	Learners seek to acquire competence to cope with the demands of their world; they seek personal development and achievement of potential; they also seek immediate gratification; learning must be immediately applicable.

Source: Malcolm S. Knowles (1980) *The Modern Practice of Adult Education: From pedagogy to andragogy*, pp.43–44. Reprinted by permission of Prentice-Hall, Inc., Englewood Cliffs, New Jersey.

2   Self-directing individuals occasionally need support. The role of the trainer is to recognise when this exists and to provide the appropriate support, either personally or using group members.

3   Whenever possible, the experience of each individual must be tapped. To deny a person's experience is to deny that person. The probing of experience from people with different backgrounds so that they may learn from each other is one of the fundamentals of Action Learning, which has been applied with notable success in problem-solving situations in industry and is now being used as the basic methodology in management development programmes up to and including the MBA.

4   The participative method should be widely used on training programmes because:
    – it utilises members' experience for the benefit of others, including the trainer
    – it is only by having an experience that people begin the experiential learning cycle, which is outlined later on
    – involvement in an experience ensures that the span of attention is widened so the participants learn more
    – by participation in an experience, participants not only gain knowledge and skill, but also have certain feelings and emotions that can be a powerful way of changing attitudes and can give them greater self-insight and greater insight into others.

5   The content of a programme should be a contract between trainer and learner. This meets the learner's needs for relevance to the present and moves away from the principle of deferred gratification, which is unacceptable for most adults. The involvement of the learner in deciding programme content also increases commitment because he or she part-owns the decision.

6   Where knowledge is imparted with the delegate in the passive mode, there should be ample opportunity to reinforce the learning by varying methods. Reinforcement is a vital part of the learning process and methods used should differ according to subject material and individual learning styles. Variety stimulates and makes the learner more receptive.

To summarise: according to Knowles, the andragogical model is a *process model*, not *a content model* that has been employed by traditional education. The andragogical tutor is a facilitator, a consultant, a change agent, who prepares in advance a set of procedures for involving the learners in a process of:

■   establishing a climate conducive to learning

■   creating a mechanism for mutual planning

- diagnosing the needs for learning
- formulating objectives and therefore content that will satisfy these needs
- designing a pattern of learning experiences
- conducting these learning experiences with suitable techniques and materials
- evaluating the learning outcomes and rediagnosing learning needs.

The process model does not ignore content – rather the emphasis is on providing procedures and resources for facilitating the learner's acquisition of information and skills. This ownership by the delegate of the programme objectives and content increases commitment, harnesses his or her intrinsic motivation and is a powerful way of influencing attitudinal change. If it serves only to influence his or her attitude to training and make it more positive, that in itself is a powerful achievement.

Experiential learning theory

This relatively recent theory has much in common with other theories – eg cognitive theories – and has its roots in laboratory training and T-groups. It puts the emphasis on the actual experiences that people go through as the starting point for the learning process, and then emphasises the analytical mental processes that individuals use to analyse the experience. Feelings are also part of any experience which, if explored and analysed, can help increase self-insight. In short, experience when allied to analysis can bring about behavioural change.

The model is not only an important theory of learning but is extremely useful as a means of explaining individual differences in learning style. In the 1970s David Kolb developed the Experiential Learning Cycle, stating that there are four distinct stages in the learning process, and that each individual has a preference for a particular style of learning.

Kolb developed his experiential learning theory, seeing it as an integrated process in four main stages:

1 Learning begins with a 'here and now' experience. This could conform to existing views or contradict them.

2 This experience is followed by a collection of data and observations or reflections about that experience.

3 There follows a continuation stage involving analysis of the data, when we begin to conceptualise and commence the internalisation process of what has been learned from the experience.

4 There is then the final stage, at which we modify or alter our behaviour. We enter a stage of experimentation and test the new knowledge or concepts to see if they work in practice.

Kolb's circular learning pattern is shown in Figure 14. When one 'revolution' has been completed, the cycle begins again.

Kolb developed beyond his theory arguing,

> ❝ as a result of our hereditary equipment, our particular past life experience and the demands of our present environment, most people develop learning styles that emphasize some learning abilities over others. ❞

He then developed a Learning Style Inventory in order to measure an individual's relative emphasis on each of the four learning abilities. He named the four basic styles *converger, diverger, assimilator* and *accommodator.*

An alternative description of learning styles was produced, along with a questionnaire, by Peter Honey and Alan Mumford in 1983 (2nd edn, 1986). They described the four basic styles as *activist, theorist, reflector* and *pragmatist,* each one largely corresponding to each of the four stages in their learning cycle. The emphasis is on preference in the way an individual learns, which could have significant implications in the design and methodology used in training and development programmes. Furthermore, it is not believed that one's preferences are incapable of change — basic

Figure 14 Kolb's Learning Cycle

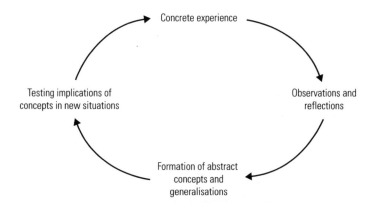

Source: 'Towards an applied theory of experiential learning', in *Theories of Group Process* by D. A. Kolb and R. Fry (1975), Wiley. Reprinted by permission of John Wiley & Sons Ltd.

style can change but requires, first, self-awareness of one's strengths and weaknesses, and second, a commitment to change. Whereas the responsibility for the former rests with the trainer, responsibility for the latter rests firmly with the learner. An ability to develop one's weaker styles of learning can result in a significant level of personal development for many individuals. (A more detailed description of Honey and Mumford's four learning styles, along with their learning cycle, is given in Chapter 5.)

A good example of how the theory can be applied is in learning how to improve at a sport such as cricket, golf or tennis. The trainee is likely to go round the learning cycle many times, using a variety of methods such as individual tuition, demonstration and coaching, practice, reading, watching others, receiving feedback from a video, reflecting and analysing his or her game and playing in a competitive situation. Such a variety of training methods will take the individual around the learning cycle many times over, which will reinforce earlier learning.

Although the trainer can utilise the Learning Styles questionnaire to determine the composition of the group, it must be remembered that it will offer no guarantee of successful group learning. Other variables, such as interaction among group members and facilitation style, can have a significant impact on determining whether learning outcomes are positive or negative. Nevertheless, such an instrument can be invaluable in increasing individual self-awareness and also in helping the trainer to choose the appropriate training method.

Experiential learning theory underpins a method now increasingly used in management training, namely Action Learning. This method was pioneered by Revans with such organisations as the National Coal Board and GEC, and it utilises the group as a resource for solving real-life work-related problems. Individuals (called 'fellows') form a group ('set') to address and solve problems and implement solutions. Such sets usually run for a minimum of six months and have attached to them an external facilitator, or set adviser, whose primary role is to offer an expert input of knowledge in an academic discipline relevant to the project in order to help the set focus on the key issues and guide the set appropriately towards project completion.

Both end product (outcome) and process are thus important learning vehicles for participants and make significant contributions to an individual's capacity to learn how to learn.

Learning to learn and self-development

The recently emerging trend away from teaching to learning has gathered increasing momentum. Consequently, attention has focused more and more on how to equip the learner with the strategies and range of learning styles that not only are appropriate for present learning but also are transferable to future learning situations. Individuals must recognise that opportunities for learning are all around them and that experience must be fully utilised and processed.

Learning is not a static or one-off event. It is a continuous process, and we need to know what to do, how to do it, and when to act – and part of that process is adapting new strategies and strengthening existing styles, however weak. Learning to learn, therefore, is at the very heart of self-development.

Two definitions of 'learning to learn' will help clarify the concept further. First, Mumford defines the four major elements as:

- helping managers to know the stages of the learning process and blockages to learning

- helping managers to understand their own preferred approaches to learning

- assisting individuals in making the best use of their existing learning preferences, or building additional strengths and overcoming blockages

- helping individuals to carry their understanding of learning from off-the-job to on-the-job opportunities.

Second, Smith defines learning to learn as: 'possessing or acquiring the knowledge and skills to learn effectively in whatever learning situation one encounters'. However, he does stress that there is probably no such thing as a 'complete learner' – so, for example, someone may be effective when learning independently, yet be ineffective in the classroom.

Opportunities for learning are probably greater now than ever before. In addition to learning from everyday experience, the opportunities provided by new technology, such as computer-assisted programs, are enormous.

It would probably be useful at this point to describe briefly the work of Allen Tough at the Ontario Institute of Education. His research in 1970 revealed that the typical adult conducts about eight learning projects in one year, and that the average person spends about 100 hours per project or 800 hours every year.

It may well be that the number of hours devoted to learning projects will have increased since 1970, given the increased commitment of organisations and managers to continued development and the need for constant retraining and updating because of the ever-increasing pace of change. It is important that adults optimise their learning from this scheduling, whatever the commitment. Learning how to learn is vital to the success of this process. Confidence in learning breeds competence in learning and is a great motivator to future learning. Furthermore, both individuals and organisations need to look beyond the present and to the future, and individuals need to be empowered to take responsibility for their learning as part of a continual process of development.

Mental processes

New technology has made a great contribution to our understanding of the brain. Sophisticated equipment – such as brain scanners – has increased our understanding of the physiology and functioning of various areas of the brain. This section looks at memory and outlines the different functions of the two hemispheres of the brain. It is also becoming clear that the potential of the brain is almost unlimited and that we only use a fraction of that potential. The number of possible combinations, interconnections and thought processes in the brain probably exceeds the number of atoms in the universe! By utilising our knowledge of learning and a number of new techniques, we can begin to make greater use of that potential.

Memory

This term is usually used to describe the activities of acquiring, retaining and recalling information at any time. It has been viewed as a faculty capable of being exercised and improved, rather like a muscle, in order to improve the quantity and quality of what we learn.

There are several kinds of memory:

- visual – it is this aspect of memory that those possessing a photographic memory exercise
- auditory
- kinaesthetic – this refers to movement memory and is utilised in sport, touch-typing or any activity that requires muscle co-ordination.

When we use our memory, the process of recovery is called *remembering*.

We have two types of memory (irrespective of the kind of memory): short-term memory and long-term memory.

Short-term memory (STM) is a temporary store of a small amount of information. Information entering the STM is either quickly lost or transferred to the long-term memory (LTM).

The STM has a very limited capacity. As a rule of thumb, we can ordinarily recall seven items – objects, letters, numbers – arranged at random. For example, write the following sequence of numbers on a flipchart and ask a group to remember them. If successful, after each group, move on to the next group. See how far you get.

Try	1367
Then try	14859
Then try	278643
Then try	78563142
Then try	836723195

You can improve this skill in either of two ways:

- by the process of 'chunking' which involves grouping items into chunks numbering no more than seven. The technique is widely used in learning subjects like typing or morse when items (dots, dashes, letters) are brought together and learned in groups

- by arranging items in a meaningful way. The following two exercises exemplify this.

Exercise 1.
Write the following list of numbers on a flipchart, give the group 20 seconds to memorise the list, and then invite them to remember it.

714212835424956637077849198

The delegates will not be able to recall this sequence unless they realise that it is the 7 times table, which will facilitate recall.

Exercise 2.
Write the following sentences individually on a flipchart. Give the group 20 seconds to memorise each sentence, and invite them to write it down.

LPB ODN QRX GKT KRZ UCF JMA ISW
THE BIG FAT CAT SAT ON THE MAT

The implication of this exercise for the trainer is that meaning assists memory and we can remember very little of what we do not understand.

This addition of meaning is the main reason for the use of *mnemonics,* which are extremely useful in examinations. Provided there are not too many of them, they are a most useful aid to memory. Two examples will serve to show their use. (Both arise out of helping my own children while taking public examinations at school.)

Example 1.
Ask students to recite in chronological order the main geological time periods from the Cambrian to the Pleistocene. Although they may be familiar with most of the periods,

they will probably not be able to name the sequence correctly. Equip them with the mnemonic 'China Owls Seldom Deceive Clay Pigeons, They Just Chase Each Other Making Preposterous Puns', and it becomes much easier. The first letter of each word in the sentence is the first letter of a geological period, the names of which the students will become very familiar with.

Example 2.
Ask students to list the ten minerals in order of hardness from talc to diamond. The mnemonic 'The Girl Can Flirt And Other Queer Things Can Do' makes memorising them much easier. Students will be familiar with the names of each of the minerals through practical, hands-on experience.

Recall is facilitated by rehearsal such as rote learning. Those of us who repeated our multiplication tables in our formative years or who regularly use a telephone number are often capable of impressive acts of memory. The more the cycle is repeated, the more likely the information is to pass to the long-term store. There probably lurks in our LTM many a telephone number, car registration number, post or zip code, capable of being recalled following regular usage in the distant past.

Long-term memory (LTM) usually contains information that is more permanent, and the process of transfer from the STM to the LTM is assisted by revision or repetition. Also, the less the distraction or interference during a session of learning, the more chance that the information will be committed to long-term memory. The following quotation from Dale (1968) aptly summarises the situation:

> For material to enter long-term storage it has to survive an initial period during which retention loss can be extremely rapid. In order to survive, the amount of material should be small; it should be as free as possible from inter-item acoustic confusions, it should be varied so that interference between successive messages is minimised; also an opportunity for a brief period of silent rehearsal should be provided after each component message is presented.

There are three essential processes in the long-term memory:

- encoding – the process of passing information from STM to the LTM. It is probable that the information passes through several levels of processing, such as visual/auditory, syntactic and semantic, to be stored in either non-verbal imagery or in verbal syntactic form

- storage – the capacity of the memory is enormous, especially when we consider the amount of information and experience we utilise every day

■ retrieval – information stored in the memory is retrieved when appropriate as part of the process of remembering, and often in great detail. Whether anything committed to the LTM is ever completely forgotten is, for the moment, unclear. Occasionally, something lodged deep in the LTM resurfaces after a trigger or stimulus.

Visualisation

Research has now revealed that the brain has two distinct halves which have different functions and very different ways of processing information. The two halves are linked by the *corpus callosum* which is also used to send messages from one side of the brain to the other. Although the two halves do function together, research with patients in whom the link is severed has revealed that the two halves can function separately, without communication between each other.

The specialisations of the two sides of the brain are shown in Figure 15. It is not yet certain how the two halves are co-ordinated. Neither half has a monopoly of a particular cognitive style, the functions differing mainly in degrees of emphasis. There are implications arising from this phenomenon for the trainer:

■ An awareness of this split in brain function, and of one's own strengths and weaknesses, is required.

■ It is possible to develop the weaker half of the brain. There are a number of techniques and exercises that can be used to develop both sides and brain interaction, which can constitute a self-development project. Most of us tend to

Figure 15 Front view of the brain and its main functions

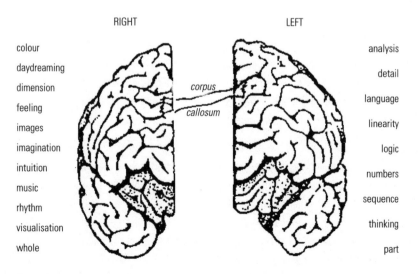

RIGHT   LEFT

colour   analysis
daydreaming   detail
dimension   *corpus*
feeling   *callosum*   language
images   linearity
imagination   logic
intuition   numbers
music
rhythm   sequence
visualisation   thinking
whole   part

have a stronger or more well-developed half, and very few of us can claim the complete development and effective use and co-ordination of both halves. So-called geniuses like Einstein and Leonardo da Vinci are often quoted as good examples of people with well-developed left and right brains.

■ The trainer should attempt to utilise both brain hemispheres of delegates on courses and in other training activities. So case studies using logical interpretation, along with visual aids, imagery and sensory stimuli that will appeal to the right side of the brain, should be used to enhance the impact of the message and achieve greater internalisation.

Emerging horizons

In this final section, two new developments are summarised briefly: Accelerated Learning and Neuro-linguistic programming.

Accelerated Learning

Rose (1991) suggests that the average human being uses only 4 per cent of his or her potential brain power, saying that in many westernised countries we have inherited a culturally-imposed legacy of limiting individual learning and development. Much of this is a result of the way we are taught to learn in the school system. The main emphasis is on developing left-brain functions through verbal and deductive subject content. In addition, in organisational life and in society, we tend to place higher value on logical and analytical thinking rather than on intuitive and artistic ability. Independence of thought and creativity are not usually given high recognition. We thus starve the right side of the brain of development and, therefore, limit the whole brain's potential.

Accelerated Learning methods attempt to stimulate the whole brain, not just one hemisphere, and emphasise the role played by our emotional state in learning because it produces a higher state of arousal, thereby increasing the chances of retention. Also, if we feel good, we are more receptive to inputs through the various sensory pathways. To make use of the whole brain, there is a need not only for logical thought but also for imagery, because visual association assists memory.

With Accelerated Learning techniques, use is made of a variety of sensory pathways – visual, auditory, kinaesthetic, participation and doing. In helping an individual to learn a foreign language, the learning material thus provides visual aids (books), auditory aids (cassettes) and encouragement to imitate various physical actions or gestures demonstrated in an accompanying video – vocalisation is also encouraged by all media. In short, total involvement of the individual and both sides of the brain are utilised and encouraged wherever possible.

Neuro-linguistic programming (NLP)

This new development followed work in the USA in the 1970s by a linguistics specialist, John Grinder, and a mathematician, Richard Bandler (1979). They made a comprehensive study of excellent practitioners in interpersonal communication, identified the key factors contributing to this personal excellence, and produced a model for one-to-one communication to assist others (combining the skills of mathematical notation and linguistic analysis).

NLP is now increasingly being used in education, training and development. In addition, more recent work by Robert Dilts (1983) and Grinder has extended the scope of NLP to leadership and the management of groups and organisations. NLP states that an individual's concept of reality is his or her own subjective interpretation, as the mind acts as a filtering mechanism. Each individual's interpretation is influenced by his or her experiences and attitudes relating to other people and the surrounding world. From birth, every individual learns to programme his or her reactions and develop strategies that become internalised and are lodged in the unconscious mind, and then become automatic. There are two kinds of strategies:

- those involving language

- those relating to body movement.

By studying excellent performers, the researchers developed a framework to help an individual identify his or her own strategies and those of others. In short, it helps to increase self-awareness and awareness of other strategies. From heightened self-awareness, an individual can choose whether to continue with present automatic responses and behaviours or begin a process of change.

NLP uses many different techniques, some of which relate to self-management. An example of this is 'outcome thinking', which requires the subject to go through a number of stages:

- thinking of a positive outcome associated with a certain situation and continually rehearsing it by imagining it through as many senses as possible

- identifying the personal resources, such as confidence, required to bring about a positive outcome and finding those resources using stimulus-response techniques. The S-R techniques require the individual to think of a time when he or she possessed the required resource, to relive the emotions experienced then, and to recall how that state was achieved in order to help recreate it.

- rehearsing the use of the required resources in the new situation to try to ensure a positive outcome.

Such techniques have been used by sportsmen and women either to help to achieve success or to avoid getting embroiled in future on-field troubles. For example, soccer players with a short temper, who have been dismissed from the field for retaliating to verbal and physical provocation, are asked to visualise alternative responses in order to avoid future trouble. Trainers also could use this technique to improve their own performance in the many areas associated with delivering or facilitating training.

So in the past 100 years our knowledge and understanding of the learning process has increased enormously. No one theory can adequately explain the complex processes of learning in all situations. Furthermore, more than one theory of learning is often applicable in a single situation. Many of the more recent developments in the field incorporate some of the work of the early learning theorists.

EXERCISES

1   Consider two good and two poor learning experiences.
    (a)   Why were they good?
    (b)   Why were they bad?
    (c)   What did you learn from them in terms of the principles of adult learning?
    (d)   From your answers to these questions, how can you apply your learning points to your own training events?

2   Consider each of the groups of learning theories that have been outlined in this chapter. From your own experience, can you:
    (a)   think of a situation when it formed the basis of the learning strategy?
    (b)   evaluate whether it was effective in helping the trainer to meet his or her objectives?

3   Consider a number of training situations in which you might be involved in the near future. Which learning theory or group of theories should influence your design of the training situation?

4   For each of the groups of learning theories described, consider situations when they should be key influences on the training method employed.

KEY POINTS

Major points in this chapter include:

- There are three major types of learning that bring about a change in behaviour: cognitive (knowledge), psychomotor (physical skills) and affective (attitudes and values).

- Adults learn very differently from children, and the training methods must take account of these differences.

- Participative learning, with the emphasis on process, is becoming more widely recognised and used, and differs greatly in its approach from traditional education.

- People have different styles of learning, which should be recognised in course design.

- The adult's self-directing need to learn shows that many people seek learning opportunities beyond the confines of a formal course.

- In the years ahead, individuals will need to be empowered to learn how to learn.

- Repetition and reinforcement are important parts of the learning process.

- People can improve the retentive and creative capacities of the brain by using a number of well tried and tested techniques.

FURTHER READING

ALDER H. (1993) *The Right Brain Manager*. London, Piatkus.

ALDER H. (1994) *NLP: The New Art and Science of Getting What You Want*. London, Piatkus.

BANDLER R. and GRINDER J. (1979) *Frogs into Princes*. London, Real People Press.

BEARD C. and WILSON J. P. (2001) *The Power of Experiential Learning. A Handbook For Trainers And Educators*. Aldershot, Gower.

DALE H. C. (1968) 'Memory and effective instruction', *Aspects of Education*, 7, 8–21.

DILTS R. (1983) *Applications of Neuro-Linguistic Programming.* Cupertino, California, Meta Publications.

HARRIS T. L. and SCHWANN W. E. (1961) *Selected Readings on the Learning Process.* New York, Oxford University Press.

HONEY P. and MUMFORD A. (1982) *A Manual of Learning Styles.* Maidenhead, Peter Honey.

HONEY P. and MUMFORD A. (1986) *Using Your Learning Styles.* 2nd edition. Maidenhead, Peter Honey.

INGLIS S. (1994) *Making the Most of Action Learning.* Aldershot, Gower.

KNOWLES M. S. (1975) *Self-Directed Learning.* Chicago, Association Press/Follett.

KNOWLES M. S. (1980) *The Modern Practice of Adult Education: From pedagogy to andragogy.* Chicago, Follett.

KNOWLES M. S. (1984) *The Adult Learner: A neglected species.* 3rd edition. Texas, Gulf Publishing.

KOHLER W. (1973) *The Mentality of Apes.* International Library of Psychology, London, Routledge.

KOLB D. A. (1984) *Experiential Learning.* Englewood Cliffs, New Jersey, Prentice Hall.

KOLB D. A. and FRY R. (1975) 'Towards an applied theory of experiential learning', in COOPER C. L. (ed.) *Theories of Group Process.* New York, Wiley.

MALONE S. (2003) *Learning About Learning.* London, Chartered Institute of Personnel and Development.

McGILL I. and BEATY L. (1992) *Action Learning: A practitioner's guide.* London, Kogan Page.

MEGGINSON D. and PEDLER M. (1992) *Self Development: A facilitator's guide.* Maidenhead, McGraw-Hill.

MUMFORD A. (1980) *Making Experience Pay.* Maidenhead, McGraw-Hill.

MUMFORD A. (1986) 'Learning to learn for managers', *Journal of European Industrial Training*, Vol. 10, No. 2. Bradford, MCB University Press.

O'CONNOR J. and SEYMOUR J. (2002) *Introducing Neurolinguistic Programming.* London, HarperCollins.

PEDLER M. (1991) *Action Learning in Practice.* 2nd edition. Aldershot, Gower.

REVANS R. W. (1971) *Developing Effective Managers.* Harlow, Longman.

REVANS R. W. (1982) *The Origins and Growth of Action Learning.* Bromley, Chartwell Bratt.

REVANS R. W. (1983) *ABC of Action Learning.* Bromley, Chartwell Bratt.

ROGERS C. (1983) *Freedom to Learn.* Columbus, Ohio, Merrill.

ROSE C. (1991) *Accelerated Learning.* Aylesbury, Accelerated Learning Systems.

SKINNER B. F. (1953) *Science and Human Behaviour.* New York, Macmillan.

SKINNER B. F. (1972) *Freedom and Dignity.* New York, Knopf.

TOUGH A. (1979) *Adults' Learning Projects. A Fresh Approach to Theory and Practice.* 2nd edition. Toronto, Ontario, The Ontario Institute for Studies in Education.

WEINSTEIN K. (1998) *Action Learning: A practical guide.* 2nd edition. Aldershot, Gower.

5 ▪ COURSE MEMBERS

Any course is sure to be composed of a wide variety of individuals.

After reading this chapter, you will:

- be aware of the range of expectations of individuals
- be familiar with several theories of motivation and be able to describe several things that motivate people
- know all about four major styles of learning
- be able to utilise the above information to influence the design of your training course.

EXPECTATIONS

Whatever the level of involvement in training or educating adults, one thing can be guaranteed: you will be faced with a varied group of people. Part of your task is to mould this diverse unit into an effective and working group so that they go away having learned something and in a positive frame of mind.

When one analyses the diversity of the group in such terms as intelligence level, motivation, skill, experience, culture, etc, one wonders how any group can ever become an effective unit – the task facing the facilitator is daunting and sometimes appears overwhelming.

The task of welding a varied group into an effective learning unit is one of the great challenges – and this is why, when success is achieved, training and working with adults is such a rewarding and stimulating experience.

Some of the individual differences that exist (eg motivation) are examined later. It is the role of the trainer to be aware of them. It is also the role of the trainer to have some awareness of the delegates' expectations – and here there are some common elements.

They often expect to be taught in the old-fashioned way

Many attendees are prisoners of their early educational experience. They are steeped in the old-fashioned, forceful and rigid methods. They view the educational process as something that must be endured. If they are actually enjoying it, then they feel guilty.

Many years ago I ran a short course entitled 'Introduction to Psychology'. Free from the constraints of an examination syllabus and in receipt of feedback from the students on the topics that were of interest, I designed and delivered a programme. Experiential, participative methodology was widely used; 'chalk and talk' was kept to a minimum. The rate of fall-out was small and, towards the end of the course, the participants enquired about the possibility of a follow-up. We sat down to discuss it – and it was then that one middle-aged lady asked me, 'Are we going to be doing some serious work, or are we going to carry on just messing about?' She had enjoyed the course but felt guilty that she hadn't endured the process!

As a postscript to this anecdote, a follow-up course was designed and delivered, the middle-aged lady attended, and we continued to 'mess about'. And everybody enjoyed it!

They expect the trainer to display the appropriate professionalism

Attendees expect appropriateness in several areas:

- *knowledge of the subject* – Unless you really are, you are not expected to be the world's greatest authority, but some form of expertise is expected. And if you don't know the answer, ask the group – one of them may know

- *knowledge of, and possession of some skills in, teaching and facilitation* – With the vast range of learning methods available, no one expects you to be totally at ease with all of them. Know your strengths and your weaknesses, and make the appropriate adjustments

- *standard of dress* – A sloppy image and appearance do not characterise a professional person. I am not advocating the wearing of formal dress, but one can dress smartly without being formal. It is in this area that appropriateness is important. If one is delivering a management training course in-house, some formal attire is usually the order of the day; if the course is delivered away from base, then smart, casual dress seems to be *de rigueur*. Appropriate dress is one aspect of the norms that a group sets itself, and the trainer has to be aware of it and give it consideration in deciding what is appropriate.

It is amazing what delegates observe about trainers, and one should never underestimate this ... as the following anecdote reveals.

One of the problems in our household is that we have a washing machine that devours socks. It is very discriminating, because it devours only one sock in every pair so that at the end of a week I can be left with numerous socks that do not match.

On a trip to a Mill Shop in the north of England, I discovered a large consignment of plain, fawn-coloured socks. They were on sale at 5p a pair, and so – with an eye for a bargain – I duly bought 20 pairs. I reasoned that not only would they colour-match most of my casual attire, but they would also defeat the voracious appetite of the household washing machine, because they were all the same. No longer would I be left with a pile of socks that didn't match.

At this time I was delivering a 'Train the Trainers' course which met every Friday evening for three hours for three months. I wore casual attire that I felt was appropriate to the informality of the group sessions.

On the last evening of the course it was agreed that we should finish with a wine and cheese function. Because this was a little more formal I decided to dispense with my casual attire for the evening and wear a navy blazer, and collar and tie.

At the end of the session, we adjourned to the corner to begin the eating. As I poured the wine for the participants, one turned to the other and said, 'Good Lord! He's at last changed his socks!'

Moral: nothing goes unnoticed!

They expect to be made to work

This counters the strong belief of those who think that participants attend for a social reason or that they will stay away if taxed.

People come to learn – and if they are not stretched, they will usually vote with their feet. On management development programmes it is often perceived that delegates are going off for a rest. This could not be further from the truth. While there is no denying that the facilities and hospitality of modern-day conference centres are a source of enjoyment, they are usually a source of refreshment and mental replenishment at the end of a long day. If the course menu is not relevant and well presented, the delegates – who are only too aware of the costs to the company of attending programmes – will go back to work.

They expect to be treated with dignity

Participants expect to be treated in a dignified and respectful manner. They do not expect to be talked down to. They expect to be treated as equals, although they will respect the role, and therefore group leadership, of the tutor. Although that is brought with them, such respect and trust has to be earned by the tutor.

Adults are as vulnerable as children – they dislike harsh criticism, humiliation, neglect and being patronised. This vulnerability is derived from the fact that they want their adult status to be recognised. If adverse feedback has to be given, it should be done on a one-to-one basis in private, and should focus not on the person but on the behaviour of that person. (For more detail, see Chapter 6.)

MOTIVATION

It is important, before looking at some theories of motivation, that a distinction be made between 'intrinsic' and 'extrinsic' motivation.

Intrinsic motivation is the internal drives that an individual experiences (the 'push from within', which is self-generated). *Extrinsic motivation* is concerned with incentives (objects external to ourselves which act as a 'pull from without').

In the training situation, some of the factors that could affect an individual's level of extrinsic motivation are trainer style, learning environment, learning methods, individual and group support, praise, recognition, etc. If one accepts the belief that the adult is strongly self-directing in his or her desire to learn, then the role of the trainer is merely to harness that intrinsic need. The extrinsic, motivating methods do not 'switch on' the learner – they either 'switch off' or increase the drive.

In many human situations – at work; at school, in dressing rooms, etc – one often hears the question, 'How do I motivate my people?' Unfortunately, there is no panacea – every situation and every individual must be treated differently. Numerous theories have been propounded on this subject, of which the best-known are:

- Hierarchy of needs (Maslow), 1954
- Hierarchy of needs (Alderfer), 1972
- Socially acquired motives (McClelland *et al*), 1976
- Two-factor theory of work motivation (Hertzberg), 1966
- Theory X and Theory Y (McGregor), 1960
- Expectancy theory (Vroom), 1964.

These theories of motivation are all aimed at the occupational field and are included in the content of very many management development programmes.

It is not the intention here to describe all the models in detail. Countless books have been written on the subject, and any reference library should have them. Rather, the intention is to outline two of the theories: those of Maslow and McClelland.

These have been chosen because they have a more direct relevance to the training situation than the others. In a learning situation, everyone has a variety of needs and most of these needs are covered by the theories of Maslow and McClelland. The trainer must be aware of these needs, and must understand the implications for the training situation. An exercise focusing on how we, as trainers, can meet those needs follows after the outline of the two theories.

Maslow's hierarchy of needs

Maslow stated that every human being has certain *basic* human needs, and he arranged them in an order, a hierarchy (see Figure 16), such that the needs become more human as one proceeds up the hierarchy, or up the pyramid, as shown in the diagram. Maslow distinguished the basic needs in the order of their importance (prepotency) – so physiological needs must be satisfied before safety needs which, in turn, must be satisfied before love needs, and so on. Progress through the hierarchy is more likely once the important basic needs have been satisfied, because satisfaction of a need usually leads to the emergence of the next higher need.

The main divisions of the hierarchy are:

- *physiological needs* – The basic needs of the human being are for food, liquid, oxygen, warmth, shelter, etc. They do not include sexual needs because sex is seen as more important to the survival of the species than to the survival of the individual.

- *safety needs* – These are higher needs than physiological needs. People need security and safety from threatening objects, or situations. These needs are most evident in young children, whose development is generally helped by a stable home background and undisruptive routine.

- *love needs* – These assert themselves only when physiological and safety needs have been gratified. Most human beings need both to receive and give affection. They also need to belong (sometimes called the 'herd instinct'), which in turn satisfies their safety needs. In a group situation, people can often be made to conform because of a possible threat of isolation, while in society people who do

Figure 16 Maslow's hierarchy of basic needs

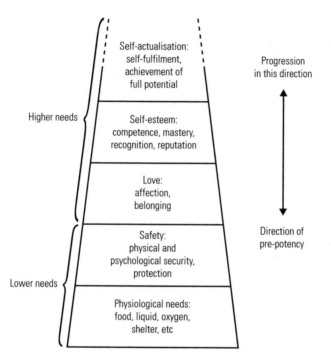

Source: Motivation and Personality, 2nd edn, by Abraham H. Maslow (1954), Harper & Row, © 1970 Abraham H. Maslow. Reprinted by permission of the publisher.

not conform to the norms of behaviour risk being labelled 'drop-outs', and pressure to conform can be quite intense.

- *self-esteem needs* – These exist at two levels:
  - desire for competence, achievement, independence, *confidence in oneself* in front of others, etc
  - desire for prestige, status, recognition, importance, *appreciation by others*
- *self-actualisation needs* – The desire to fulfil one's potential (`What a man can be, he must be'). Self-actualisation is dependent on self-realisation, because we need to know what we can do before we know if we are doing it correctly.

Linked with basic needs, but forming their own hierarchy, are what are termed the *cognitive* needs. The search for knowledge (curiosity needs) and the understanding of that knowledge so that we may possess an understanding of the world in which we live is a basic human motivator. Often, the satisfaction of the cognitive needs enables the satisfaction of the basic needs to take place, and in fact the two are often mutually dependent on each other.

The three primary social motives

These are based upon the work of David McClelland and are:

- the need for achievement
- the need for affiliation
- the need for influence or power.

The need for achievement

This is the need for measurable personal accomplishment. People high in this need seek out challenging or competitive situations and establish realistic and achievable goals. The concerns of a person with a high need for achievement are:

- *to outperform someone else* – The individual's primary concern is to engage in an activity in which he or she can win or do better than others: for example, winning a race, doing a better job.

- *to meet or surpass a self-imposed standard of excellence* – Often this self-imposed standard of excellence does not involve competition with others, but is a self-imposed standard of high-quality performance, for example doing an excellent job, finding a better method. The emphasis is not so much on quantity or output but on working hard to achieve excellence.

- *to make a unique contribution* – The individual is concerned with having an extraordinary rather than an ordinary accomplishment, and in utilising unique or innovative methods to achieve success.

- *to set long-term goals* – This involves the setting of goals beyond the immediate future, often up to five or ten years ahead.

The need for affiliation

This is the need for being with someone else and/or enjoying mutual friendship. The concerns of a person with a high need for affiliation are:

- *to be part of a group or team* – The individual enjoys being on the team, sacrifices his or her own needs for the good of the team, and enjoys the relationships and companionship that group activities can bring

- *to be liked and accepted* – The individual wants to establish, restore or maintain a close, warm and friendly relationship with others

- *to maintain positive interpersonal relationships* – The individual expresses an emotional concern about separation from another person and indicates a desire to restore a close relationship that has previously existed.

- *to be involved with people in the work situation* – The individual talks about people and working with people as the main focus of his or her occupational life.

- *to minimise conflict* – The individual takes steps to avoid conflict and endeavours to establish harmonious interpersonal relationships. This may involve restoring harmony to different relationships.

The need for affiliation is about the concern of establishing, maintaining or restoring a positive emotional relationship with another person. The relationship is most adequately described by the word 'friendship'.

Certain interpersonal relationships by themselves are not indicative of a need for affiliation. For example, mother–daughter, father–son, husband–wife, etc, are all descriptions of a relationship between two people, but they do *not* necessarily mean that the participants in the relationship have a high need for affiliation or, indeed, that the relationship has the warm companionable quality indicated in the definition of need for affiliation. These relationships must be further characterised by a concern about maintaining or restoring a positive relationship.

The need for influence or power

This is the need of the individual to attain an 'influence goal'. The concerns of a person with a high need for influence (or need for power) are:

- *to acquire a reputation or position* – The individual is concerned with public evaluation. The concern is for positions of high status, to influence the cause of events, and about his or her reputation and the judgement of others of his or her powerful position.

- *to be in control of situations* – The individual is concerned with controlling people and situations. He or she will seek positions or situations where this control can be attained and exercised.

Sometimes the individual will attempt to influence or manipulate by strong or forceful actions, such as verbal attacks or by giving support or advice that has not been requested. Or there may be an attempt to control another person by regulating their behaviour or the conditions of their life.

Analysis of the models

The two models outlined focus on the individual *needs* of the learner. Below are listed a series of needs from the two models. Write down at least one thing a trainer can do to meet each need in the participant so that he or she has a positive effect on the learning process.

- achievement
- affiliation
- influence
- physiological requirements

- security
- self-directedness
- self-esteem
- self-fulfilment.

Some answers are suggested below.

Achievement

(a) We set tasks that are neither too easy nor too difficult so that the learners feel a sense of achievement. 'Step-by-step' or 'bite-sized chunks' is the order of the day.

(b) We recognise their achievement by giving positive feedback. While we recognise our own achievements, achievements that go unrecognised by others over a period of time have a demotivating effect.

Affiliation

We make the individual feel at home by making him or her part of the group – ie we reduce any feelings of isolation. We allow ample opportunities for interaction to take place between group members, both during the course and in socialising during out-of-course hours.

Influence

We give ample opportunities for participation. Syndicate work, individual presentations, co-counselling – all give individuals with a power need the opportunity to assert themselves.

Physiological requirements

We ensure that the learning environment is appropriate – the right temperature, the right amount of light, low levels of noise. If the course is residential, that facilities are good, particularly the food! If there are feelings of discontent about this, delegates cannot focus their minds fully on learning.

Security

We strive to make individuals feel at ease by reducing tension and anxiety. They must never feel threatened or exposed. We therefore encourage group interaction and counsel individuals, if appropriate, to create an informal, relaxed, but purposeful atmosphere.

Self-directedness

We give them the opportunity of setting their own learning objectives and, where appropriate, choices in the way in which they learn.

Self-esteem

We make people feel good about themselves. We give them tasks that are stretching, but ones in which they have a good chance of success. We praise and recognise their accomplishments. We give feedback. We never put them down or destructively criticise. If criticism is needed, we allow them to recognise the flaw themselves so that they accept the criticism and will probably commit themselves to improvement. Process reviews using CCTV are a good way of achieving this.

Self-fulfilment

We give them the opportunity to set their own goals. We support them in an appropriate way to achieve those goals.

DRIVE AND PERFORMANCE

Most people are goal-oriented. They strive to achieve. The role of the trainer is thus to harness the drive that this need activates, and not to turn it off.

We must therefore ask the question, 'Is there a connection between the amount of drive present and the behaviour that it generates?' Is it merely a question of increasing the drive in order to increase the performance? Or is there a level at which performance tails off, beyond which an increase in drive will have no positive effect? And what are the differences between individual learners and their capacity to deal with stressful situations?

These are not easy questions to answer. Experiments with rats in 1908 by Yerkes and Dodson indicated a relationship between the level of motivation or arousal and the difficulty of the task. This is shown in Figure 17.

If the level of arousal is nil, then the performance is nil. As arousal increases, so does performance, but only to a certain point – beyond this the performance drops. The

Figure 17 The Yerkes-Dodson law

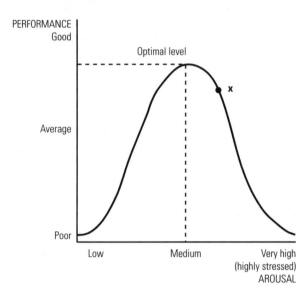

theory suggests that we all have an optimum level of arousal that produces an optimum performance. As we reach a state of high arousal – anxiety, stress, even fear – our performance drops. Anyone who has taken a driving test will remember that although they were highly motivated, their levels of anxiety may have produced a below-par performance (point **x** in Figure 17).

It follows, therefore, that there may be a relationship between the difficulty of the task and the level of arousal which, in turn, affects performance. A simple task requires little arousal, so performance is low. At the other end of the spectrum, a performance requiring a quantum leap which is beyond the capability of the individual induces no motivation and no performance. Who is motivated to achieve when they know they cannot possibly do it?

The implications of this model for the trainer are:

- Tasks must be set which are neither too simple nor too difficult, because both lead to reduced motivation, for different reasons.

- the climate or atmosphere in the training room must be neither too stressful nor too laid-back. The trainer's own anxiety level (too high or too low) will contribute significantly to this level, because we often project our anxieties and attitudes on to others.

LEARNING STYLES

In the previous chapter the experiential learning theory developed by Kolb was outlined. Kolb went beyond his theory, arguing that

> ❝ as a result of our hereditary equipment, our particular past life experience and the demands of our present environment, most people develop learning styles that emphasise some learning abilities over others. ❞

He then developed a Learning Style Inventory in order to measure an individual's relative emphasis on each of the four learning abilities. In his view there were four basic styles, which he labelled *converger, diverger, assimilator* and *accommodator.*

The Learning Style Inventory attracted considerable criticism and was followed in 1982 by the Learning Styles Questionnaire (Honey and Mumford). This was designed to help individuals discover their preferred learning style(s) so that they could select learning experiences most suitable to their style of learning.

As with Kolb, the LSQ was linked to a four-stage cycle of learning from experience (see Figure 18). The four learning styles relate to the four stages in the cycle in this way:

■ A preference for the *activist* style equips you for Stage 1.

■ A preference for the *reflector* style equips you for Stage 2.

Figure 18   The Honey and Mumford Learning Cycle

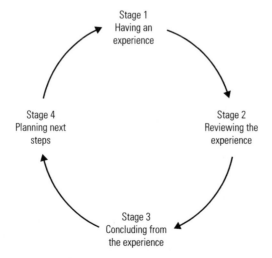

- A preference for the *theorist* style equips you for Stage 3.
- A preference for the *pragmatist* style equips you for Stage 4.

The four styles, with a brief behavioural description, are:

Activists

Activists learn best from activities in which they encounter new experiences/problems/opportunities. They enjoy the here-and-now and often thrive in short-term crisis situations. Change, a fast pace, and a range of diverse activities to tackle, provide an essential stimulus.

They are usually extrovert individuals who enjoy a high-profile position and the stimulus of challenge. Being thrown in at the deep end with a difficult task is viewed as a challenge, not a daunting or overwhelming hurdle. They love to 'have a go'. Routine and longer-term consolidation have little appeal.

Reflectors

The preference here is for a more 'back-seat' role. Reflectors like to stand back on the edge of activity and observe what is going on from different perspectives. They are usually good at data collection and make a thorough analysis in their own time before coming to conclusions. They like to consider the situation from all angles before acting, and so usually they are cautious. Pressure and tight deadlines are not welcomed.

Theorists

Theorists like concepts, models, theory, systems, and the opportunity to explore interrelationships and associations. They like to be stretched intellectually, and because they prize logic and rationality, they tend to have analytical minds. Such an analytical preference may mean that they prefer to work on the edge of things – ie from a detached position – rather than be involved from within the situation.

Pragmatists

A preference here indicates an orientation towards relevance between subject matter and one's own position. 'If it works, it's good' is the motto, and pragmatists look for the earliest opportunity to implement what has been offered. They are practical down-to-earth individuals who enjoy problem-solving and making practical decisions. The focus is very strongly on implementation and output.

Learners who score high on all four styles are best equipped to deal with all stages of the learning cycle, but the majority of people display distinct preferences, with undeveloped styles. The development of these undeveloped styles can form a very useful self-development exercise. There are many advantages in broadening your range of learning skills. As an individual you can learn much more from everyday experience, while as a trainer you are likely to appeal to and help a wider range of delegates – and so become a more effective trainer.

If there are significant individual differences in learning styles, then there are some essential implications for the trainer. Knowledge of learning styles can:

- be used in a training situation to give an individual feedback on learners' preferences and to assist them in planning their own learning opportunities. It may also help them to increase their range of learning

- give an objective input into the construction of learning groups

- enable trainers to refine and improve their understanding of learning skills

- give trainers objective information about the composition of a group so that they can tailor the methods used to suit the learning styles of the participants.

EXERCISES

Remember that there is an exercise on page 82 relating to individual needs and two theories of motivation.

1   Obtain a copy of the Learning Styles Questionnaire. Complete it, and consider your feedback.
    (a)   What are your learning strengths?
    (b)   What styles do you need to develop?
    (c)   Draw up your own action plan to develop your ability to learn.

2   Consider the learning methods best suited to a group of:
    (a)   activists
    (b)   reflectors
    (c)   theorists
    (d)   pragmatists.

3   How would you best design a course and choose the methods best suited to a group composed of members with a variety of preferred learning styles?

KEY POINTS

Major points in this chapter include:

- Adult students have a wide range of expectations, many of which result from the conditioning process in their formative years.

- Adults have a wide variety of needs which, if harnessed, provide strong motivation for learning. An understanding and recognition of the needs by the trainer can accelerate the learning process.

- From the training standpoint, motivational theory and adult learning theory are closely related.

- Recognition of different styles of learning can help plan courses and assist individual development.

FURTHER READING

ALDERFER C. P. (1972) *Existence, Relatedness and Growth.* New York, Free Press.

HERTZBERG F. (1966) *Work and the Nature of Man.* Cleveland, Ohio, World Publishing.

HONEY P. and MUMFORD A. (1982) *A Manual of Learning Styles.* Maidenhead, Peter Honey.

HONEY P. and MUMFORD A. (1986) *Using Your Learning Styles.* 2nd edition. Maidenhead, Peter Honey.

KOLB D. and FRY R. (1975) 'Towards an applied theory of experiential learning', in COOPER C. L. (ed.) *Theories of Group Process.* New York, Wiley.

MASLOW A. H. (1954) *Motivation and Personality.* 2nd edition. New York, Harper & Row.

McCLELLAND D., ATKINSON J. W., CLARKE R. A. and LOWELL F. A. (1976), *The Achievement Motive.* New York, Irvington.

McGREGOR D. C. (1960) *The Human Side of Enterprise.* New York, McGraw-Hill.

VROOM V. H. (1964) *Work and Motivation.* New York, Wiley.

YERKES R. M. and DODSON J. D. (1908) 'The relation of strength of stimulus to rapidity of habit formation', *Journal of Comparative Neurology and Psychology*, 18, 459–82.

6 ■ LEARNING METHODS

The object of any training event is involvement. The greater the involvement of the learners in the learning process, the greater is the learning.

After reading this chapter, you will:

■ be able to describe a range of participative learning methods

■ know how to select the most appropriate method to increase learning

■ know when and how to use psychometric instruments and to give feedback.

Many years ago a group was shocked when they realised that there is not always a direct connection between teaching and learning. Just because someone is teaching, there is no guarantee that learning is taking place.

Nevertheless, the prime objective of any teaching session is to help participants learn, and to achieve this objective it is necessary to adopt the appropriate method. Numerous factors can impact upon the choice – and these include:

■ the nature of the information or skill to be learned

■ the size of the group

■ your own strengths or preferences as tutor

■ the resources available, including time.

The third of these points is not as selfish as it first appears. If you choose a method you are uncomfortable with, you will probably give a below-par performance, with negative impact on the learning of your delegates.

In choosing a learning method, it would be appropriate to remind ourselves of some of the principles of learning outlined earlier.

- Your students must be ready to learn. Students learn best when they feel a need for the material presented.

- You must provide an opportunity for your students to *practise* the information or skill you present. The more they work with the material, the better they can do it (*reinforcement*).

- Provide the opportunity or explore ways in which they can use the information or skill you present. Individuals learn best when they can experience success with the material. This increases both self-confidence and motivation.

There is a wide variety of learning methods available to help your participants learn. Unfortunately, no one method or combination of methods can be applied with equal success in all circumstances. You will have to experiment with several different approaches to find the right one for a particular session.

One very good way is to watch someone else do it. In all walks of life we are always looking for new and better ways of doing things, and training is no exception. Identification with, and imitation of, a fellow professional – particularly a very experienced one – is a powerful way of learning and increasing your own professional competence.

You will also have to develop the ability to decide whether you present information to the whole group or to small sub-groups. Presenting information to a large group is useful because you can:

- give the same information to everyone at one time

- provide for group interaction

- help individuals work co-operatively towards a common goal

- save time.

Presenting information to a small group is time-consuming, but you can:

- be more aware of individual needs and be more specific in meeting those needs

- be more aware of individuals' understanding of your material and any learning difficulties they are experiencing

- more easily pace your presentation to an individual's learning speed.

Often you will give information to a whole group and then work with individuals or small groups to reinforce your material. Sometimes you can use individual group members to facilitate small group work. Peer facilitation can be a very powerful learning aid as well as a very easy way of coping with large tutor:student ratios.

THE RANGE OF LEARNING METHODS

Lecture

One of the earliest thoughts of many people who consider a career in the training field is that they have to become lecturers. They feel they must strive to become inspirational orators in front of an audience, and if they cannot, they will not be successful. This is undoubtedly due to tradition and their experience of higher education, where the lecture was the predominant mode of instruction.

Many students, as a result of their earlier educational experiences, also expect it and feel most comfortable with it – it is familiar, it is easy to 'hide' in a passive audience, and one rarely is challenged or has to confront difficult issues.

Consequently, the lecture is probably the most widely-used method in training, although in recent years, with the increasing emphasis on participative methods, its importance has been reduced. Like all the other teaching methods, it is extremely effective when used at the right time and delivered in the appropriate way.

Lectures have the following disadvantages:

- They proceed at one pace, and that pace is determined by the lecturer. This is unlikely to suit everyone in the audience.

- Because the interaction is one-way, feedback is difficult.

- They are a strain on the weak, short-term memory capacities of adults (see Figure 19).

Figure 19 The attention span of a group

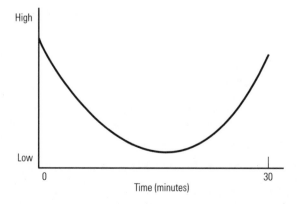

- They require a special kind of self-confidence. 'All eyes are on you' – and the longer the lecture continues, the more your mannerisms, voice, etc, will be scrutinised and critically appraised, often to the detriment of your message.

Despite these disadvantages, when do we use the lecture? As a general rule of thumb we use it when we have to give a mass of information to a large group, and this is the most economical use of time. Appropriate occasions might be when we are:

- developing a background for the course in the opening session
- presenting material to introduce a topic
- presenting material supplementary to assignments.

How can we ensure that we become competent lecturers?

- Strive for the highest degree of informality that can be achieved without losing the respect of the delegates.

- Stand up when talking and occasionally move back and forth in front of the group.

- Be aware of the attention span of the audience (see Figure 19). Psychologists tell us that during a 30-minute presentation the attention curve steadily drops from an early high to a low after 20 minutes, before returning to the early high (presumably when the lecturer indicates the end is near). This has the following implications for the lecturer:

  - Keep your presentation short – 15 to 20 minutes is probably as much as most adults can absorb.
  - Change the pitch, tempo and volume of your voice when speaking.
  - Try every device you can think of to add variety, spice and surprise to your presentation. Some of the presentation graphics packages may help add more visual stimulus and interest, so investigate their potential.
  - Make the key points either very early or very late.

- Eliminate distracting habits and mannerisms and always maintain eye contact with a cross-section of the audience.

- Have a clearly defined beginning, middle and end. This helps you in the delivery, and it also helps your students.

To sum up, the lecture has a very important part to play in imparting information to a lot of people quickly. In terms of structure, 'Tell 'em what you are going to say; tell 'em; then tell 'em what you have told them.' It is best used in short bursts with frequent recourse to alternative, participative methods.

Demonstration

Often the best way to get your point across is actually to show or demonstrate what you mean. This can be done by a demonstration *per se* or as a reinforcement or follow-up to a lecture. The way in which one tackles it may depend on the complexity of the operations or principles. Generally, the greater the level of complexity, the more you will have to build the demonstration *into* the lecture so that students can watch as you demonstrate. This requires extensive use of actual items or visual aids.

The demonstration method is useful because it:

- attracts and holds individuals' attention
- is easily understood
- is convincing – it is 'here and now', and imitation is a powerful way of learning
- ties together theory and practice.

The drawbacks of demonstration are:

- Things can go wrong. But by ensuring that you are competent at the task and have prepared thoroughly, you increase the chance that it will be 'all right on the night'.
- It is often difficult to ensure that everyone can see what you are doing.
- Everyone has to be present. This problem could be overcome if you make a video tape of your demonstration with appropriate close-ups. This ensures that you can reinforce whenever you want, as well as overcome the problems of absent members or those unable to see clearly.

During the demonstration you should:

- describe your objectives and procedures clearly
- show each step slowly and carefully, relating past experiences to future steps
- check on your effectiveness and the students' understanding by asking questions
- encourage participants to ask questions
- supplement with literature, models or other visual aids
- summarise key points
- show other applications of the skills or process just presented.

Follow up each demonstration:

- Give participants the opportunity to practise the skills or process just demonstrated.

- Give individual/group help during practice sessions. Often you can use more competent members of the group if your own resources are stretched.

- Raise questions to clarify points.

- Praise and recognise success – a great motivator and confidence builder!

- Help individuals recognise the application of what has been learned to their real-life situations – ie facilitate the transfer of learning.

In any training where the emphasis is on *skills* you will use the demonstration method frequently. In terms of the structure, tell them what you are going to do, tell them how to do it, let them practise, and tell them, and praise them when they can do it.

Discussion

The discussion method is an excellent means of covering the essential points of a session and meeting objectives while allowing individuals to ask questions, raise issues, etc, with everyone else in the group. Sometimes it can be woven into the lecture – in which case the trainer can go beyond the previously recommended 15–20 minutes.

When leading a discussion, you should ask questions that serve to provide a general exchange of ideas or facts. It is also a good way of drawing out conflicting opinions. Usually you will find that most adults are willing and anxious to contribute their opinions, even to the point of disagreeing with the leader. This results in interesting and lively discussions which are bound to make more lasting impressions than merely lecturing and giving out facts.

When using the discussion method, keep it under control and on the subject – and guillotine it at the right time. In other words, you must ensure that pertinent matters are emphasised and that the time is not monopolised by any particular topic or individual. Too often the discussion degenerates into a free-for-all. To manage a discussion successfully the leader needs an astute sensitivity to the group and its dynamics, which involves very different skills and approaches from those required for lecturing and demonstrating.

Active, participatory methods

Four main methods are examined here:

- case study
- role-play

- simulation

- games

Although these are distinctive methods in their own right, there is some overlap. They are all participatory methods with the objective of enabling participants to learn general principles through involvement in a situation as similar to real life as possible. They tend to be used most widely in the field of management training and development, and involve a much higher degree of risk for everyone. Often CCTV can be used for giving in-depth feedback and assisting the coaching.

Case study

With this method you present the specific details of a problem, usually in written form, and ask the participants to suggest the best solution they can, based upon the given facts. They must also be prepared to discuss not only their proposal but *why* they reached their decision and, sometimes, *how* they reached their decision. Interesting and varied solutions usually emerge, and if several groups tackle the same problem, interesting comparisons can be made which can be shared in a plenary session.

The case study requires:

- lengthy preparation time and may need a couple of dry runs to fine-tune (but be prepared for the comment that there is never enough information!)

- the facilitator to be familiar with the material – which should not be a problem if he or she developed it

- clear and concise briefing for participants

- debriefing and summarising skills so that the main points are shared with everyone.

Role-play, simulation and games

These may be used to bring together knowledge and experience and to show their interrelationship. They are used widely in skills training – for example, in interviewing, conducting meetings and customer care. Group members are assigned certain roles and are required to work through a problem or situation by acting it out while in character. Sometimes the information used is in the form of a case study.

Role-play becomes a simulation if it is carried out continuously and intensively over a longer period of time using elaborate materials, and if fresh problems and complications are introduced periodically.

In management training, business simulations may take place over days rather than hours, management teams receiving feedback on their decisions and progress from computers.

Sometimes these teams are in competition with others and the exercise could be termed a game.

The advantages of simulations are that they:

- are an enjoyable way to learn if they are realistic

- require active involvement from participants

- bring academic subjects alive so that the gap between theory and practice is bridged

- give participants the opportunity to experiment in 'low-risk' situations, where there is no fear of retribution and where as much can be learned from mistakes as from successes

- are very adaptable to groups of mixed ability, and distinctions between bright and less bright become blurred

- make it difficult for participants to remain aloof and uninvolved because the enthusiasm of group members is contagious and levels of motivation rise

- encourage peer facilitation and support because the most able can support the least able

- increase awareness of participants' own behaviour and the effect on others

- improve interpersonal skills, team skills and the ability to process information to solve problems and to confront and handle conflict.

Disadvantages include:

- Role-play can degenerate into horseplay when individuals exaggerate their perception of their role. A firm hand may be required to remind the group of the objective(s) or to bring the role-play to a halt. Once this method gets out of hand, you will find it difficult to get a group ever to take it seriously again.

- Lengthy preparation and several dry runs are required.

- It can be very expensive, either because of preparation time or hiring/purchasing charges. Some of the more elaborate business simulations can cost several thousand pounds.

- It involves a high degree of risk. Once the exercise is under way, it may well not proceed in an orderly, predictable fashion. The role of the facilitator becomes that of a co-ordinator. Some may feel very uncomfortable with the loss of control.

- Participants may invest high levels of energy and emotion in the process, which can get out of hand. A high level of sensibility is required, and external interventions may be needed.

- Sophisticated equipment may not function predictably, so that credibility suffers.

- It requires a lengthy debrief or process review, which can make exhausting demands on time and facilitator skills.

- It needs clear and concise briefing for participants, which may require long periods of time.

- Where teams of tutors are required to run elaborate simulations, clashes of philosophy and style can occur.

Open learning

Sometimes called 'distance learning', this form of learning has enjoyed successful and spectacular growth over the past 30 years. Institutions such as the Open University and the National Extension College have all made significant contributions to open learning.

There is no universally agreed definition of open learning. It is based on the belief that it is a way of opening up new opportunities for people to learn at a distance from the providing organisation.

It usually involves the use of specially prepared self-instructional materials (packages). These are often expensive to produce and buy. Such packages come in modular form, and each module can be studied on its own or as part of a sequence in which they then form a complete course. Learners work through the modules on a step-by-step basis, and study or completion time can vary from a few hours for a single module to months for a complete course.

Open learning packages may utilise a variety of teaching media – from printed material, through audio and video material, to practical work and computer-based training (CBT). Learners usually work through the package on their own, but they may meet together with other learners from time to time, plus have access to occasional tutorial or counselling support.

Open learning is one answer; it is not the complete answer to many individual and organisational training needs. Its main advantages are:

- It is very flexible in how it can be used. 'Anytime, anywhere' often applies, and it can be used to train very large numbers. It can thus offer economies of scale, so reducing the cost per trainee and therefore overall costs.

- It can offer 'just-in-time' learning if you are using a package, in that it is there when you need it.

- Organisations with few or no training resources – for example, small and medium-sized enterprises (SMEs) – can 'plug into it', if externally provided, to develop their people.

- There are no geographical limits to provision and participation.

- Little time off work is required, which has a particularly strong appeal to the small-business employer and employee.

- It meets the self-directed needs of the adult learner.

- The modular structure aids the assimilation process, as students progress at their own pace and there is opportunity for reinforcement. This is especially true if support or coaching and/or mentoring is available.

- It is less threatening because there is no group exposure. This can have a strong appeal to those whose lack of formal education has undermined self-confidence.

There have been many impressive achievements through open learning by those with little formal education, often of mature years, which has resulted in improved self-confidence and job competence. The relatively low cost of tutorial support can make it a cheaper alternative to other forms of learning.

Major disadvantages of open learning include:

- Some of the packages, especially in the field of CBT and interactive video, are extremely expensive. Cost/benefit analysis is required before investment is made.

- Good time management skills and study habits are required, which many students may not possess, especially if they have had little experience of study.

- The learner is isolated. Many open learners suffer from a lack of support, so that lack of recognition can have adverse motivational effects. Consequently, some programmes experience a high drop-out rate. This is an important hidden cost consideration – a course that is initially cheaper than a traditional course because of absence of tutorial support is more expensive if there is no completion or end product. Potential open learners should check on the support available – from the institution, their organisation and their family – before committing themselves.

- The lack of group involvement ensures little or no peer support or group identity. It also means that one rich resource for learning – namely, the experience of the adult learner – is rarely used. Opportunities to share, compare and advise with peers are limited.

■ There are very few people whom you can put in front of a computer and leave them to get on with it. PC skills are unlikely to be high among older trainees, and this in itself can cause considerable resistance to training. It is therefore vitally important to identify the IT-literate and technophobes before going down an open or e-learning route.

Open learning can be a useful addition to a company's overall training strategy. It can never replace the traditional group approach, but for some subject areas it may be an appropriate and cost-effective way of meeting individual and organisational needs. In almost all cases, the learner must know that there is back-up in tutor form and be regularly tested/challenged on what he or she is learning.

Using IT in training

Information technology has mushroomed spectacularly in recent years, particularly with the growth of the World Wide Web, and has had an enormous impact upon our lives at work and at home. Inevitably, it has influenced the training field, in some cases for the better and in others with detrimental results. As with all training aids, IT aids can be a help or a hazard – their success depends largely upon how they are used and managed. This is no different from dealing with people, and so rather than discuss in detail different forms of IT and how to train with them, I propose to list briefly some of the major principles that should be borne in mind with regard to training with new technology.

Among the types of IT that may be of use are:

■ word processors

■ desk-top publishing

■ computer-based training (CBT) and various refinements of CBT

■ viewdata

■ interactive video.

People must be trained in their use, and their successful operation should ensure the production of high-quality training materials.

Three key points for the trainer to be aware of when using IT are:

■ Most trainees working with new technology have little interest in the technology itself. They are not interested in technical specifications or how it works. Their chief interest is 'What will it do for me?' Once they are sold on the benefits, they are interested only in how to use it and how quickly they can acquire the required skills. The focus on the benefits, therefore, needs to be firmly on the applications of the technology for the job.

- Many older trainees may be frightened of new technologies. They see IT as threatening and an assault on the status quo. This is less so with younger trainees, who have recently emerged from an education system in which access to various forms of IT has been an everyday event.

- Younger trainees, however, may well be dismissive of low-quality IT-based programmes because computer games and movies have exposed them to extremely slick and sophisticated graphics and they may well judge these packages on their appearance rather than on their content.

- The technology is a means to an end, and is not an end in itself or a justification for the learner's attendance.

I once attended a management meeting in which those present were urged to follow a course of action 'so we can help the computer'. Mistaken priorities, perhaps – I had always believed the computer existed to help the trainees!

Some tips for the trainer in terms of method:

- Make instructions simple. How many instruction books and manuals have you read that were written for the expert rather than for the novice? Technical jargon clouds understanding and produces alienation and turn-off.

- Make initial tasks simple (user-friendly) to overcome the 'technology resistance' barrier.

- Build simple tasks sequentially – ie 'chunk' them.

- Do not patronise the learner, particularly an older one.

- Provide plenty of support, especially in the early stages of tuition. Remember that this can be easily managed if you use the more able members of the group.

- Give regular feedback on performance. This should be built into the programme and also come from the trainer and assistants.

- Let trainees progress at their own rate. Let *them* force the pace – not you or the programme.

- Make everything as interactive as possible.

- Make training with the new technology a fun experience. A half-day spent watching youngsters using IT in junior schools may be a very worthwhile experience.

Note: readers are strongly advised to read Chapter 4, *Learning theory*, to discover the justification for some of these tips – and particularly the sections *A process model of adult learning*, *Experiential learning*, and *Memory*.

E-learning

E-learning comprises a wide variety of specialist technologies, although they all have one thing in common: delivery by electronic methods. These include, but are not limited to, the Internet, an intranet and CD-ROMs. E-learning is here to stay, and it should be part of a strategy for learning in an organisation. It is *not* a panacea for all learning needs and training interventions. Although e-learning is good for knowledge-harvesting, dissemination and management, areas such as soft skills training do not really lend themselves to electronic delivery. It should therefore be viewed as another tool in the bag for the trainer.

Experience to date in numerous organisations suggests that it usually works best when it is blended with traditional forms of training. The advantages and disadvantages that apply to open learning and were noted earlier in this chapter apply equally to e-learning. Consequently, it is *how* a trainer tackles the difficult task of blending both approaches that is the key to e-learning success. When designing and delivering an e-learning or blended learning approach, all the principles outlined in this book for designing and delivering classroom training still apply.

E-learning will never replace classroom training – it is a means of enhancing rather than replacing existing training programmes. It is also not for everyone, and organisations must provide appropriate support for e-learners once they have started to train online. Although blended learning works best, such blended solutions are not easy to put together, and organisations and trainers should *think about the learning process first, and the technology second*. Jumping on a bandwagon just because it is trendy may mean that effective organisational learning solutions are not achieved.

However, some companies have been successful in integrating e-learning with their existing programmes, and this has enabled e-learning to reinforce learning concepts, and has broadened the classroom experience by putting learners in touch with others facing similar learning situations, as well as enabling them to access extra support services.

There have been some impressive in-company programmes that have combined Action Learning with e-learning. The use of electronic methods – e-mail, the World Wide Web, chat rooms, noticeboards, networking, electronic courseware, etc – when combined with the powerful process skills of an Action Learning programme, has produced some powerful personal development experiences, while the implementation of organisationally related work projects has given the organisation a considerable return on its investment.

If successful e-learning is to be implemented, the following are essential:

- excellent learning design

- reliable software

- e-tutor support

- face-to-face mentoring

- facilities to involve learners in online discussions so that they do not feel isolated and instead do feel part of a group with an identity

- providing an in-house mentor whose role is to allocate time and resources to enable learning to take place; who will provide encouragement and support for the e-learners; who will liaise with the e-tutor(s); and who will train and liaise with other in-house mentors. E-learners should not be left isolated – otherwise, as with other distance learning provision, they may drop out early and derive little benefit from a programme, and the method fails to become cost-effective.

Conclusion

The ability to choose the right method for the job is the work of the professional, and is part of the set of skills you must develop as you become a competent trainer.

Research indicates that learners retain about:

> 10 per cent of what they read
> 20 per cent of what they hear
> 30 per cent of what they see
> 50 per cent of what they both hear and use
> 70 per cent of what they say
> 90 per cent of what they say and do.

This is shown diagrammatically in Figure 20. Although these percentages are only approximations, they do indicate that:

- participants learn faster by seeing and hearing than by hearing alone

- participants learn even faster when doing is added to seeing and hearing

- participants retain more of the things they do than of the things they are told.

Figure 20 Learning approaches and relative information retention

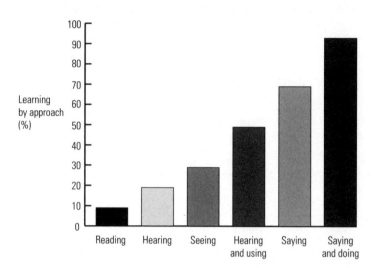

This breakdown reinforces the effectiveness of some of the more recent developments in learning theories, such as experiential learning theory and accelerated learning, which are outlined in Chapter 4.

By carefully considering your objectives and the nature of the material you plan to cover, you can select the most effective technique or combination of techniques for each session. In the last analysis it is your decision. Some techniques can be used in many different situations; others are appropriate only occasionally. The more methods you have in your repertoire, the easier it will be for you to meet your objectives, and the more likely it will be that you will do a better job. Widening your repertoire is a lengthy process, involves risk-taking, and is part of your personal development in achieving training competence. Good luck on your journey.

PSYCHOMETRIC INSTRUMENTS

Increasingly in recent years psychometric instruments have been used on management development programmes. This section focuses on their use in training and development, rather than in other areas of application such as selection and succession planning.

The main areas of use for psychometric instruments are:

- as a tool for self-awareness to assess relative strengths and weaknesses, and to give feedback on managerial and/or leadership style

- as a means of building teams, assessing strengths and weaknesses and constructing more effective units of complementary personality types
- as a way of looking at interpersonal relationships in groups to discover why group processes are undermining the effectiveness of the group.

One advantage of using psychometric instruments is the flexibility they offer in terms of administration and application. They can be completed before a course, or during a session; the results can be fed back to the delegate either on a one-to-one basis or in a group situation; and the feedback from them can be reinforced by a variety of methods, particularly in a residential setting where the mind can focus on learning at an intensive level. More is said about this last advantage below.

Group presentation and feedback

In dealing with the instructions for completion, receipt of completed questionnaires, scoring and giving feedback, the format can vary. Generally, the more complex the instrument, the greater is the time taken to ascend the learning curve; also, the greater is the depth of feedback so that there will be a requirement for the delegate to come to terms with it before rejecting or accepting it.

With a complex instrument, such as some detailed personality inventories available, the following format has been largely successful:

1 Questionnaires and answer sheets are given to participants before the course for completion and return. In addition to going over the test instructions, the following points are emphasised:
  (a) it is a self-report instrument
  (b) there are no right or wrong answers
  (c) delegates should always think of answering the question in terms of context – work, home, etc – and should therefore consider the feedback in the context in which they completed the questionnaire.

2 Answer sheets are scored and profiles plotted, and feedback may be written before the group presentation takes place.

3 During the presentation, delegates are asked to rate themselves in terms of the style, type, etc, that is being covered by the talk.

4 Individuals are given feedback from the scored questionnaire.

5 With the group's permission, results are shared and comparisons made between:
  (a) individual types in the group
  (b) the self-ratings that they carried out during the presentation.

Note: Receipt of such feedback requires an atmosphere of openness and honesty because the individual sometimes has to confront himself or herself. It is usually appropriate for the facilitator to share some personal feedback with the rest of the group.

6   Reinforcement takes place through various methods:
    (a) reading
    (b) co-counselling interviews with others on the programme, particularly delegates' 'more opposite' type
    (c) behavioural observation of others during the course, especially during practical tasks
    (d) behavioural awareness of self – for example, by observing CCTV playback.

Individual feedback

Sometimes this has to take place on a one-to-one basis. The feedback should be viewed as developmental, not as a judgement or criticism, and the end goals should be:

■ ownership of the feedback by the individual

■ a commitment to change, where appropriate

■ some discussion, however preliminary, of follow-up action as part of the individual's development.

The feedback is a participative exercise, so that everything that is done should be viewed and felt as helpful. This means that the feedback should be carried out in a relaxed atmosphere, free from tension, and characterised by openness and honesty.

Like any interview, it is important to devote time to establishing a rapport. This could be over either a relatively short period of time or a longer period. Experience will tend to suggest when the time to move on has arrived. Having sensed that the point to move on has been reached, the following sequence may be appropriate:

1   Explain the test and say how the feedback will be given. It is often useful to reiterate some of the points made at the time the test was administered.

2   Give the feedback:
    (a) Be authentic (open and straight) and non-evaluative.
    (b) Do not take a 'critical parent' role (see page 136).
    (c) Check for understanding by getting the individual to state back what is being said.
    (d) Allow time for resistance (some ideas may take time to get used to).

(e) Do not become defensive yourself. It is often useful here to use phrases such as:

> 'The profile indicates that …'
> 'You have reported on yourself that …'
> 'The indications are that …'

not

> 'You are …'
> 'One area of weakness is …'
> 'This is a poor score on ….'

3   Work with the positives.

4   Discuss indicated weaknesses or development points:
    (a)   explore solutions and/or actions
    (b)   consider benefits
    (c)   explore possible avenues for development
    (d)   obtain (if appropriate) a commitment to change, but remember that responsibility for this should rest with the individual
    (e)   check whether any support – eg access to yourself or his or her boss – is wanted.

EXERCISES

1   List some of the learning methods you have used yourself.
    (a)   Which ones do you consider yourself competent at using? Why?
    (b)   Which ones do you consider there is room for improvement on? What can you do to improve?

2   List some other trainers you have observed who were competent with various methods.
    (a)   What made them competent?
    (b)   What can you learn from them?
    (c)   List some times/events when you can experiment with new methods.

3   For each of the following methods, describe a situation in which you might be involved when it might be appropriate to use it:
    (a)   lecture
    (b)   demonstration
    (c)   discussion
    (d)   case study
    (e)   role-play

(f) simulation

(g) games

(h) an open learning package.

4 Consider a situation in which you have received feedback on yourself from a person about a psychometric test you had taken.

(a) How did you react to the feedback? Why?

(b) How did you feel about the feedback? Why?

(c) Consider how the feedback was given. What were the main learning points from it, and how can you incorporate them in your own style of giving feedback?

KEY POINTS

Major points in this chapter include:

- There is not always a direct relationship between teaching and learning.

- There is a wide range of learning methods, all with advantages and disadvantages. The role of the trainer is to select the most appropriate method in order to optimise learning.

- Participation increases the chances of optimising learning.

- Instrumented or psychometric feedback is being increasingly used in human resource development activities. A great deal of skill is required in the feedback sessions if maximum value is to be obtained from such a process.

FURTHER READING

CLARKE A. (2001) *Designing Computer-Based Learning Materials.* Aldershot, Gower.

ELLINGTON H., FOWLIE J. and GORDON M. (1998) *Using Games and Simulations in the Classroom.* London, Kogan Page.

JONES K. (1997) *Games and Simulations Made Easy. Practical Tips to Improve Learning Through Gaming.* London, Kogan Page.

MENTS M. V. (1999) *The Effective Use of Role Play. Practical Techniques for Improving Learning.* 2nd edition. London, Gower.

PONT G. and PONT T. (1998) *Interviewing Skills for Managers.* London, Piatkus.

RAE L. (1992) *A Guide to In-Company Training Methods.* Aldershot, Gower.

RUSSELL T. (1998) *Effective Feedback Skills.* 2nd edition. London, Kogan Page.

SLOMAN M. (2001) *The E-Learning Revolution: From propositions to action.* London, Chartered Institute of Personnel and Development.

THORNE K. (2002) *Blended Learning: How to integrate online and traditional learning.* London, Kogan Page.

WILSON D. (2003) *Building The E-Learning Organisation.* London, Chartered Institute of Personnel and Development.

7 ∎ MANAGING THE GROUP

People's behaviour is modified when they join a group. An understanding of how groups work can help the trainer to manage the group and increase learning.

After reading this chapter, you will:

- be familiar with some of the main characteristics of groups

- be able to describe the main stages of group development

- discern types of behaviour in groups

- identify a number of roles present within any group and be able to utilise techniques to deal with difficult group members

- appreciate some of the differences between training and facilitation

- know the major skills of good facilitation

- be able to describe some of the different styles of facilitation and their relationship to the different stages of group development.

THE CHARACTERISTICS OF GROUPS

We spend most of our lives in groups – the family, the class, the sports club, the work group, are all everyday examples. The behaviour of individuals is always affected when they find themselves a member of a group, and their relationships with different groups of people often vary considerably. Indeed, the behaviour of individuals can change dramatically when they are in a group.

A group develops a life of its own, with established conventions as to what constitutes acceptable behaviour. Within a group individuals may occupy defined positions (roles) such as 'joker', 'militant', etc, and any challenge to established positions or expectations may be strongly resented.

Furthermore, individuals who form part of a group but break the group's 'rules' are often made to conform again by a variety of means — for example, by gentle persuasion, argument, 'sending to Coventry', or whatever. Failure to conform can result in expulsion or in the individual's deciding to withdraw.

The individuals who constitute a group gradually develop shared ideas and beliefs about what the group is doing and should be doing. These ideas and beliefs, which influence individual behaviour, are termed *norms*. For example, a group at work may develop a low-output norm and any individual who works counter to this will be pressurised to conform or face expulsion — or at least lose much of the social reinforcement the group provides.

People join groups for a variety of reasons, but two generally predominate:

■ to accomplish a task — This is becoming increasingly necessary because most tasks now require an ever-increasing range of specialised skills which are fused together in multi-disciplinary teams

■ to satisfy the basic needs of the individual member: eg the needs outlined in Maslow's hierarchy (see Figure 16) — Such basic needs are usually first catered for by the family unit.

The mere existence of a group does not ensure that it will operate effectively; a group is effective only to the degree to which it is able to use its individual and collective resources. The measure of the group's effectiveness is its ability to achieve its objectives and satisfy the needs of the individuals within the group.

Sometimes the two functions are compatible with one another; on other occasions they may be incompatible, so that a conflict of interest and priorities for the individual and the group occur.

The extent to which a group can achieve success in its primary role (achieving the task) and its secondary role (social relationships) often depends on how strongly the group is bound together — ie its *cohesiveness*. A highly cohesive group is able to fulfil the task and provide opportunities for social reinforcement, whereas a less cohesive group has difficulty achieving these goals. Factors that affect group cohesiveness include:

■ *group size* — Eight to ten people can usually communicate with one another on a face-to-face basis. Beyond this number it becomes more difficult, so that sub-groups (cliques) may form that may run counter to the main group.

- *status and prestige* – A group that is respected for its efficiency and liked by others will become more cohesive.

- *proximity of working* (frequency of contact) – The greater the contact, the more opportunity exists for forging a group identity and cohesiveness. Distance brings isolation and problems of inclusion, support, and identity.

- *leadership* – The development and cohesion of a group occurs only when there is a feeling of shared leadership among all group members. This means that all group members accept some responsibility for task functions (ie those necessary to do the job) and maintenance functions (ie those things necessary to keep the group together and interact effectively).

  In a training situation, there is the complication of leadership identity caused by the role of the tutor/facilitator. Members of the group, and the tutors themselves, bring certain role expectations, and a period of mutual adjustment of expectations has to take place, particularly in the early days.

- *goals and objectives* – For any group to operate effectively, it must have stated goals and objectives. In addition, the group members must be committed to the goals. Such commitment comes from involving all group members in defining the goals and relating them to specific problems that are relevant to group members. The time spent on goal definition in the early stages of a group's life results in less time needed later to resolve problems and misunderstandings.

  In the training situation, it is suggested that the setting of objectives should be a mutual contract between learners and facilitator, and that it should be done at the start. That way there is ownership of, and commitment to, the programme objectives.

- *group climate* – This is always difficult to define, but involves effective interpersonal communication and a high level of energy. Effective interpersonal communication is about group members communicating in an open and honest manner, and requires that they listen to one another and attempt to build on each other's contribution.

  Energy is contagious, and high levels can generate enormous enthusiasm and commitment and have a synergistic effect.

  The facilitator has an enormous effect upon group climate, particularly in the early days. If he or she is enthusiastic and committed – and can communicate that to group members – there is a good chance that a positive climate will be established.

  Furthermore, the skill of listening and building on members' contributions is even more important for the facilitator, because he or she has the role of welding the group into an effective unit.

STAGES OF GROUP DEVELOPMENT

It has been well documented that groups go through several well-defined stages of development from their first meeting to their eventual disbandment.

Stage 1: 'Ritual sniffing'

This describes a newly-formed uncertain group in which the majority of members (facilitator included) are feeling uncertain and anxious. The awkwardness will probably manifest itself in a variety of defensive behaviours, such as being quiet and reserved, or outgoing and loud.

Individuals are going through a process of weighing people up. Group members are weighing up the tutor and the rest of the group, and the tutor, both consciously and unconsciously, is weighing up the group. A mental process of establishing oneself in relationship to others is evident. The concern is more with not making a fool of oneself, so here risk-taking is low.

At this stage, the role of the facilitator is to establish credibility and put people at ease. A non-threatening icebreaking activity is ideal for starting. A number of books on icebreakers are listed in the *Further Reading* section at the end of this chapter.

As the group develops there is a gradual increase in individual interaction. This can take place in the classroom or over a coffee break. Friendships and bonds are at a very superficial level and the role of the facilitator is to encourage interaction whenever possible so that deeper, more meaningful, relationships can be formed.

Stage 2: Jockeying for position

At this stage relationships develop. There is usually less tension and anxiety, and individuals begin to vie for positions of power and influence. Certain significant individuals who adopt significant roles begin to emerge.

The facilitator's job is to tune in to the dynamics of the group and the emerging roles. The facilitator must continue to earn the respect of the group, or his or her leadership may be threatened or undermined.

During this stage the group begins to decide its *modus operandi*. Important questions that are asked and addressed are:

- Who controls the group? Will it change from its early, strong dependence on the facilitator?

- How will control be exercised? Will the more authoritarian style of the facilitator be reduced, and by how much? And how will the group take responsibility for its own destiny?

- How do we deal with individuals who do not appear to be conforming to the rapidly emerging group norm? This is an important question for the facilitator – and also for the group members.

These questions must be confronted and answered if the group is to proceed. Many groups fail to find a way of dealing with their control problems and so experience 'process difficulties' which result in a less positive learning experience.

Stage 3: Getting the act together

After resolving the control issues, the group organises itself. A group identity begins to form; people are committed to the group and to each other. They want to achieve success.

At this stage the group assigns tasks, roles are clarified, and the members collaborate to support each other and solve problems. A more democratic or coaching style of facilitation is usually more appropriate for the facilitator.

This stage is usually characterised by a high energy level and commitment. Individuals respect each other, the facilitator, and their contributions, even if they do not always agree. There is a commitment to conflict resolution. New ways of doing things are explored, and the quality of listening improves if for no other reason than because the level of security is higher and the level of anxiety is lower.

There is also humour in greater abundance. People can usually laugh at themselves as well as at each other. Defensive barriers have largely been removed.

Stage 4: Maturity

Group members have forged a strong group identity and have developed rapport and closeness. Sometimes this is so strong that bonds of friendship are forged that may even last a lifetime. Members sometimes form an informal support network long after the group has been disbanded.

The group's workings are characterised by informality, humour and a high level of support for each other. People are not afraid to ask for help if they need it, and help is readily given.

At this stage it is impossible for any outsider to be integrated into the group. Indeed, the danger for a group at this level of development is that it can be so insular as to be unaware of, or unwilling to consider, outside influences that could be beneficial.

The facilitation style should now be much less directive. Sometimes the group can become so self-directing that facilitator contribution is not needed, although there is a danger that this could be perceived by the group as abdication of responsibility. It may be appropriate to renegotiate the relationship with the group, perhaps to become a process consultant to guard against complacency.

Stage 5: Old age

There is an optimum time for a group to be together to accomplish the task and meet the social needs of its members. Beyond a certain point, continuation becomes counter-productive. This stage has been reached when it becomes difficult to introduce novelty, creativity is dropping, and apathy and cynicism are beginning to set in.

If new experiences cannot be introduced or shared, it is usually appropriate to disband the group. The trick really lies in disbanding just before the rot sets in. In the same way that individuals can stay too long in a job, so groups can stay together too long so that the warm feelings and memories are erased by experience of this last stage.

Endings are always difficult. In many ways they are more difficult than making good beginnings. It is important, though, that time and energy are devoted to this process so that members 'look back with affection' rather than 'look back in anger'.

GROUP BEHAVIOUR

To analyse a small group at work, while also being a member, is a complex and difficult task. It means not only observing the group and its members but also being acutely aware of how your own behaviour (your attitudes, your physical presence, your body language, your views, etc) impacts upon others and contributes to the character of your particular group.

The field of group dynamics is complex but intriguing. An understanding of it can greatly enhance one's knowledge of self, others, and the way groups function. A knowledge and understanding of the importance of process in group workings can have enormous benefits.

Below is a list of questions that could be used to explore the dynamics of group behaviour. The questions relate to any group, and take their experience and development as the primary resources for looking at the subject. This list is by no means exhaustive and can be used in a variety of ways, and the intention is thus not to be prescriptive but to use judgement according to the situation.

1   What were your feelings when the group first met: concern, anxiety, doubt, hostility, warmth, something else? Why did you feel as you did?

2   Do you feel the same now as you did at the start? If you feel differently:
    (a)   In what way do you feel you have changed?
    (b)   What has caused the change?

3   How would you describe the atmosphere/climate within the group at this stage of the course? Has it always been the same?

4   What do you consider has been the effect of the course tutor(s) on the group?
    What do you consider has been the effect of the group on the course tutor(s)?
    What do you consider have been the effects of the course tutors on each other?

5   Do you consider that the course tutors have been accepted as members of the group? Alternatively, have they been perceived as being 'above and beyond' the group?

6   Have any members of the group taken on any particular roles? What are these roles? What have they contributed to the group?
    Who has been more 'task'-oriented?
    Who has been more concerned with the social and emotional problems of the group?

7   Has one person emerged as group leader? Or has the 'leader' varied, according to task and circumstance?

8   Do some members contribute more to discussion than others?
    Are some members reticent and shy?
    How has this been dealt with? Were the group members always aware of, and sensitive to, the needs and interests of the other group members?

9   Have members learned from each other in the group?

10   Can you identify a specific pattern of development in the group?

11   Have any sub-groups or cliques formed within the group?

12   As the group has developed and hopefully become more cohesive, has its progress affected the attitudes, feelings and contributions of individuals within it?

13   Do you consider the size, age range, sex ratio and background have been appropriate?

14   Can you think of one word that describes this group?

15   Have there been any external influences upon this group? If so, what has been the result?

16   How does this group compare with other groups that you have been involved with? What are the main differences, and why?

Dealing with difficult members

Whatever the level and whatever the subject, one thing can be guaranteed: you will have a varied group of people. To the facilitator is given the impossible task of welding them into an effective unit.

It is often the case that among the motley crew there will exist some difficult members whose behaviour taxes your group facilitation skills and can have a detrimental effect on group development and learning.

Below is a list of some of the stereotypes you might encounter, and some ways of handling them.

- *the positive type* – They are a great help in discussion, particularly when members are not very forthcoming. Use them frequently.

- *the talkative type* – Intervene tactfully and limit their speaking time.

- *the shy type* – Try to bring them into the discussion with easy questions. Always give credit wherever possible, and increase their self-confidence.

- *persistent questioners* – They will try to trap the trainer or discussion leader. Try to deal with questions tactfully and check that you have satisfied their question. Never get involved in an argument – it reduces your credibility and the group will take their side. If you do not know the answer, *admit it*. Either offer to find out after the class or ask the group if anyone can shed light on the issue. If they persist, throw it back to the group – they will usually deal with an aggressive individual most effectively.

- *the know-all or arrogant type* – Let the group deal with their theories and viewpoints.

- *the argumentative type* – Stay quiet and do not get involved. The group will deal with the problem themselves. Always try to stop them monopolising.

- *the uncooperative type* – Recognise their knowledge and experience and use them wherever possible. Be aware of their needs and play on them.

- *the thick-skinned uninterested type* – Ask them about their work or interests. They must have some! Try to relate topic matters to that and ask for a contribution. Relating it to 'where they are at' or 'coming from' usually raises interest.

- *the intellectually superior type* – Listen and consider, but do not criticise and do not be provoked. Use the 'yes – but …' technique or 'agree to disagree'. Check out what other group members think.

FACILITATION

❝ You know that I don't believe that anyone has ever taught anything to anyone. I question the efficiency of teaching. The only thing that I know is that anyone who wants to learn will learn. And maybe a teacher is a facilitator, a person who puts things down and shows people how exciting and wonderful it is and asks them to eat. ❞

(Carl Rogers, 1983)

As our knowledge of the learning process in the adult increases, and the importance of adopting an experiential approach gains increasing acceptance, a more participative approach to training has manifested itself. With this participative style, the role of the trainer has changed from that of teacher to that of facilitator.

Facilitation applies to group situations, the size of the group not usually exceeding 15. In fact, even this number can present group management problems so that a split into sub-groups may be appropriate.

Facilitation is defined by Bentley (1994) as:

❝ the provision of opportunities, resources, encouragement and support for the group to succeed in achieving its objectives, and to do this through enabling the group to take control and responsibility for the way they proceed. ❞

Facilitation is one of the key skills of a set adviser with Action Learning sets (see Chapter 4), which is the area in which the author has had most experience of facilitation. It is my intention, therefore, to use the model of Action Learning to examine:

- the three main areas of facilitation
- the main styles of facilitation
- the main skills of facilitation
- the relationship of styles and skills to the evolving group or set.

The main areas of facilitation

These are:

- *subject content* – Any group in a learning or training situation will expect to receive tuition to increase either their knowledge or their skill level. These are two of the three main areas in which we learn (see Chapter 4).

- *process* – This refers to the way in which group members decide to learn and deal with their content.

- *group management* – Every group is composed of individuals who give the group its own unique identity. The group has to decide what encouragement and support it will need, how it will proceed, and what demands it will make on the facilitator. Here, there will be a contracting process between group members and the set adviser, which will evolve over a period of time.

In Action Learning, learning is described by Revans (1971, 1983) in terms of the following equation:

$$L = P + Q$$

in which L corresponds to learning; P to programmed knowledge; and Q to the ability to ask the right questions at the right time, and to take action.

The relationship between P and Q, and also between subject content and process, is shown in Figure 21. In the author's experience, this applies equally to Action Learning sets who are pursuing either a qualification or a non-qualification programme.

As time passes, and as the set evolves, the amount of input from the tutor (initially very high) decreases, perhaps to zero. The set begins to take increasing responsibility for its own learning so that the role of the set adviser changes from subject expert and tutor to that of facilitator, and not only with regard to subject content but also – with increasing importance –to group process and interaction.

At the outset, set members may be confused, and need direction. 'Tell us what to do', 'Tell us what is required', or 'Lead us', they cry. They are passive and initially dependent. To meet these needs and to establish their own credibility, the set adviser should take

Figure 21 Learning sets

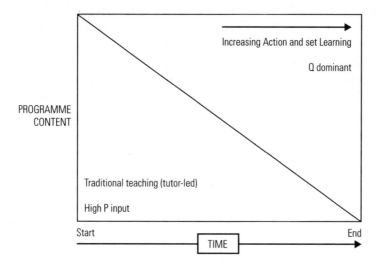

the lead and should direct and take full responsibility for presenting subject material. As the set develops, hopefully to a mature stage in which it is functioning effectively, the role and skills required of the set adviser change – from a 'hands-on' to a more 'hands-off' approach. These skills and their evolving emphases are listed in Table 2.

The objective of the set adviser/facilitator is to wean the group off its dependency so that it takes increasing responsibility for its own learning and its method of working. I would also argue that the set adviser should have two major goals which should have been achieved by the time the set disbands:

■ to produce clearly measurable outputs, in the form of work-related projects completed for presentation to the employing organisation – which has the option to implement if appropriate (so giving a return on investment in training)

■ to empower set members to believe in themselves and help themselves in the future and, from this platform of increased self-confidence, to explore and strive to reach their full potential by taking responsibility for their own learning and development.

For the facilitator, like the good parent, the ultimate objective is to hand over responsibility without fuss or trauma. From ancient China, the following quotation is most apt:

▶ Table 2 Facilitation and group development

Stage of group development	Stage 1: 'Ritual sniffing'	Stage 2: Jockeying for position	Stage 3: Getting the act together	Stage 4: Maturity	Stage 5: Old age
Facilitation style	Directive 'Hands-on'	Persuasive Influencing	Supportive Letting go	Occasional support 'Hands off'	Empowering for future self-directed learning
Facilitation skill	Content expert Leading Presenting Directing Guiding	Encouraging Challenging Questioning Probing Counselling Giving feedback 'Mirroring back'	Developing/ moving forward Listening — summarising — reflecting Focusing Coaching Tapping and developing expertise	Delegating Abdicating	Making good endings

← ——————————————— | TIME | ——————————————— →

Note: This table does not seek to suggest that particular skills are required only at a certain stage but endeavours to point out that as a group develops, facilitation skills change and evolve, with different emphases.

❝ A leader is best
    When people barely know that he exists,
    Not so good when people obey and acclaim him,
    Worst when they despise him.
    Fail to honour people,
    They fail to honour you;
    But of a good leader, who talks little,
    When his work is done, his aim fulfilled,
    They will say, `We did this ourselves.' ❞

(Lao Tzu)

Some of the ways in which the facilitator may manage the group process are addressed below.

Some skills of facilitation

These can be listed under three major headings which correspond to the three main areas of facilitation outlined earlier:

■ *subject expert* – This is important at the start of the life of the set and to help establish credibility. Skills in presentation are therefore required at this stage.

As the group evolves, this skill should be less to the fore, and the skill changes to one of recognising other expertise and knowledge in the set, and harnessing it for the benefit of all.

■ *group manager* – As the group evolves, less direction is required, and the responsibility for direction is handed over to the set. The time required for this change varies, and the facilitator should let go at an appropriate rate, according to the group's readiness to direct itself. At no stage should facilitation be equated with either control or manipulation.

The key skill that emerges relates to intervention – knowing when and how to intervene is developed only through experience. Interventions can take numerous forms, each one of them requiring a skill development, and these include:
- challenging the group or its members about outcomes or its way of working
- encouraging when the way ahead is unclear
- 'mirroring back' or summarising what has been discussed, in an objective and unbiased manner
- giving feedback to individuals and the set on the way of working or the outcomes, which may include written assignments
- counselling individuals when problems arise
- asking open and probing questions
- coaching individuals and the set
- knowing when to let go, but doing so in such a way that the set swims and does not sink.

■ *process consultant* – This mainly involves advising and commenting upon how the set operates and deals with its content and findings.

The characteristics of a good facilitator

Some of the main characteristics appear in the list below:

■ sensitivity to people and situations – this is vitally important if interventions are to be successfully made

- perception and quickness of mind
- tolerance of ambiguity
- patience
- openness, candour, and trust – this is important if a trusting and open climate is to be established within the set
- a strong desire to see others learn and develop – a good facilitator should rejoice in others' success
- empathy – being capable of 'operating through the mind of another person'
- conceptual ability
- high awareness of self
- recognition of the importance of process as well as content and end product.

EXERCISES

Reflect on some training events in which you have been involved as a trainer, participant or observer.

1 Consider a 'difficult' group.
   (a) Why was it 'difficult'?
   (b) How was (were) the problem(s) dealt with?
   (c) What could have been done differently to improve the outcome?
   (d) What are the major learning points from your observations?

2 Consider some 'difficult' individuals.
   (a) Why were they 'difficult'?
   (b) How were they dealt with?
   (c) What (if anything) could have been done differently?
   (d) What are the major learning points from your observations?

KEY POINTS

Major points in this chapter included:

- Groups are a powerful vehicle for learning.

- Groups usually go through distinct stages of development.

- A knowledge of groups and group behaviour can assist in the management (not control) of groups.

- Groups can often contain difficult members, each requiring a different method of management. Do not underestimate the power of the group in dealing with difficult members.

- Facilitation requires many more skills beyond those employed by the traditional trainer, particularly in the area of group management.

- The aim of facilitation is to encourage and give the group or set increasing responsibility for taking control of its own learning.

FURTHER READING

BEE F. and BEE R. (1998) *Facilitation Skills*. London, Chartered Institute of Personnel and Development.

CAMERON E. (2001) *Facilitation Made Easy. Practical Tips to Improve Meetings and Workshops*. 2nd edition. London, Kogan Page.

DOUGLAS T. (1983) *Groups – Understanding People Gathered Together*. London and New York, Tavistock Publications.

HEIDER J. (1986) *The Tao of Leadership*. Aldershot, Wildwood House.

HERON J. (1999) *The Complete Facilitator's Handbook*. London, Kogan Page.

HERON J. (1993) *Group Facilitation: Theories and models for practice*. London, Kogan Page.

HILLS H. (1999) *Team-Based Learning*. Aldershot, Gower.

HOGAN C. (2003) *Practical Facilitation: A toolkit of techniques*. London, Kogan Page.

HOGAN C. (2002) *Understanding Facilitation: Theory and principle*. London, Kogan Page.

HUNTER D., BAILEY A. and TAYLOR B. (1999) *Handling Groups in Action*. Aldershot, Gower.

JONES J. E. (1980) 'Dealing with disruptive individuals in meetings', in PFEIFFER J. W. and JONES J. E. (eds) *The 1980 Annual Handbook for Group Facilitators*. San Francisco, Pfeiffer (an imprint of John Wiley and Sons).

KNOWLES H.and KNOWLES M. (1972) *Introduction to Group Dynamics*. 2nd edition. Chicago, Association Press/Follett.

LAO TZU (1980) *The Way of Life* (trans. Witter Bynner). New York, Perigee Books.

LEIGH D. (1991) *A Practical Approach to Group Training*. London, Kogan Page.

REVANS R. W. (1971) *Developing Effective Managers*. Harlow, Longman.

REVANS R. W. (1982) *The Origins and Growth of Action Learning*. Bromley, Chartwell Bratt.

REVANS R. W. (1983) *ABC of Action Learning*. Bromley, Chartwell Bratt.

ROBSON M. (1995) *Facilitating*. Aldershot, Gower.

ROGERS C. (1983) *Freedom to Learn*. Columbus, Ohio, Merrill.

8 ■ THE COMMUNICATION PROCESS IN TRAINING

To be a competent trainer you must be able to communicate. The better you are at communicating, the more successful you are going to be as a trainer.

After reading this chapter, you will:

■ be able to describe the main components of the communication system and their relative importance

■ be familiar with some of the skills of effective verbal and non-verbal communication

■ know how to use some models to improve your ability to communicate.

Interpersonal communication is at the very heart of the training process. Among the Oxford Dictionary definitions are:

communicate *(verb)*: impart, transmit, share, receive
communication (*noun*): the act of imparting

Success in training is directly related to your ability to communicate. Communication is a two-way process in which information is sent, received and acknowledged, as Figure 22 shows.

Figure 22 The communication process

Types of communication that exist in the training situation include:

- oral
- written
- non-verbal (body language)
- visual
- tactile
- aromatic.

In order to receive each type of communication we need to be able to:

- listen
- feel
- see
- smell.

As Figure 22 shows, the parties have to be able to send and acknowledge messages and to change constantly from both positions.

The channel is the means by or through which the message is conveyed between the various parties. Some examples of channels of communication are the telephone (verbal), facial movements (non-verbal), personal meeting (verbal and visual), a report or handout (written), TV (verbal, visual), aftershave, perfume (aromatic), a specimen (visual, tactile), etc.

Communication is therefore a two-way process. Unfortunately, the channels can become blocked when barriers are erected. The barriers can be:

- physical – eg deafness or inability to see the sender
- emotional – eg insecurity, anxiety, feeling threatened or exposed, fear.

As trainers, we must strive to ensure that when barriers occur they are removed, and that proper communications exist. We must ensure – sometimes on our own, sometimes with group help – that the physical and emotional barriers are removed.

It is important, therefore, to stress that the competence of a good trainer requires (a) skill not only in giving information (presenting) but in receiving it, and (b) an awareness of barriers to communication and their removal in an appropriate manner.

VERBAL COMMUNICATION

You do not have to be a brilliant orator possessed of inspirational qualities to become a competent trainer. Undoubtedly, some are better at communicating than others. The objective of the communication process is clarification, not amplification, and with this objective in mind we should remember KISS – Keep It Short and Simple. Jargon, unless appropriate to the audience, should be eliminated.

Here are a few simple tips to help you improve your oral communication skills when actually presenting:

- Be relaxed.

- Smile at the audience. It is a wonderful icebreaker and it shows you are human.

- Maintain good eye contact with the whole audience. Look at them as individuals and do not stare for long spells at any one person.

- Be well rehearsed. This should aid the flow and reduce 'ers' and 'ums'.

- Be confident.

- Be credible. Establish your credibility early and never apologise for your presence.

- Be enthusiastic. Enthusiasm is contagious. If you do not believe it, how can you expect your audience to believe it?

- Be appropriately dressed. It gives you confidence, projects a professional image and demonstrates your respect for the audience.

- Be audible:
  - speak up
  - vary the pitch and avoid monotone
  - avoid the tendency to speak too quickly.

- Interact with the audience if appropriate. This can be done by asking questions and is easier with smaller groups than with large audiences. You can relate to them as individuals and use their knowledge and answers as a reference point – ie you start where *they* are at, and make your presentation relevant to *them* – and you immediately build up rapport with them.

- Be clear. Use simple, concise language and avoid jargon wherever possible.

- Use your hands and arms to emphasise points. Do not go over the top with your gesticulations and do not be statuesque. Avoid distracting mannerisms because they can become a focus of attention for the audience.

- Use appropriate humour. A well-received joke can reinforce or lighten the proceedings, but a poorly-received one can cause embarrassment for presenter and audience. Tune in to your audience first.

- Remember, everyone is nervous before presenting – but also remember that nervousness is not as obvious to the audience as to the presenter. This should help your confidence. Good preparation and rehearsal should inspire confidence. Keep in mind also that in nearly every case the audience is on your side – they want you to succeed, not to fall flat on your face!

- Vary the pace. Be aware that nerves tend to make us speak more quickly. Try therefore to err on the side of speaking slowly rather than quickly. Vary the pace, and remember also the value of silence – a pause is a very effective way of getting your audience's attention.

- Speak for an appropriate length of time. Remember the attention curve (see Figure 19 in Chapter 6) and do not go on for too long.

- Deal with questions by:
  - anticipating them
  - listening with full concentration
  - acknowledging the questioner with something like, 'Thank you. I'm glad you raised that'
  - answering as fully as possible.

Do not

- flannel – if you do not know, admit it. Either seek the answer from the group or suggest that you will find out and come back to the questioner

- put a questioner down. However stupid or irrelevant the question, do not be sarcastic or rude

- argue. Avoid confrontation and, as a last resort, agree to disagree.

NON-VERBAL COMMUNICATION

The study of non-verbal communication (NVC) or body language is a fairly recent phenomenon. Researchers have noted and recorded almost 1 million non-verbal cues and signals. Albert Mehrabian found that the total impact of a message is

7 per cent verbal (words only)
38 per cent verbal (including tone of voice, etc)
55 per cent non-verbal.

Ray Birdwhistell estimated that the average person speaks for a total of 10–11 minutes per day, and that the average sentence takes only about 2½ seconds. He endorsed the findings of Mehrabian, saying that the verbal component of face-to-face conversation is 35 per cent and that 65 per cent of communication is done non-verbally.

There now appears to be widespread agreement that the verbal channel is used mainly for conveying information and the non-verbal channel conveys interpersonal attitudes and emotions, which may or may not accord with the verbal message. It is amazing how we are often unaware that the messages our bodies are transmitting tell a very different story from our verbal message.

It is not suggested that, as trainers, we should become experts in the field of NVC. But we must be aware that body language can communicate attitudes to which the group will undoubtedly respond. By being aware of the importance of NVC, we can become much better communicators.

Conversely, we must also be aware of the messages that the individuals in the group are sending us, and which may necessitate a change in style, pace, activity, etc.

In short, we must be aware of our own NV messages and of those that the group send to us.

Here are a few tips to help you develop your ability to communicate by increasing your awareness of body language:

DO	DON'T
Keep an open posture	Cross your arms
Smile	Frown or scowl
Maintain eye contact	Look away or stare at one person
Look at the person	Point with one finger
Sit forward, if seated	Slouch in a chair, hide behind a
Have a relaxed appearance	desk or place your feet on desks
Show open palms	or tables
Keep your hands at your side	Appear tense and anxious
Hold your arms outspread	Clench your fists
with open palms	Keep your hands in your pockets
Keep your legs uncrossed	Keep your hands hidden
	Chew your pencil

Notice the importance of the eyes and the hands. The left-hand column encourages openness, trust and a relaxed, purposeful interaction; the right-hand column promotes defensiveness, mistrust, anxiety and negative interactions.

We actually project our openness or anxieties on to the group, which will respond accordingly. One problem of team teaching is that if there is an atmosphere of tension and anxiety between the team, the learning group will latch on to it and respond accordingly.

Moral: whether working on your own or with others, get your own act together first before unleashing yourself on the group.

Personal space or distance

The principle of 'territoriality' has been well established by numerous biological studies of animals. Only recently have we realised that humans, too, have spatial needs which can be affected by such factors as culture, status, role, etc.

Research by Allan Pease has indicated that there are four distinct zones that people usually maintain when communicating:

- *The intimate zone* is 6–18 inches (15–46 cm) from the body, and is the zone that we look upon as our own property. Only those emotionally close to us are permitted to enter it. This includes lovers and close family and friends.

- *The personal zone* is 18–48 inches (46–122 cm) from the body, and is the distance over which we interact at social events, particularly when we know people well.

- *The social zone* is 4–12 feet (1.2–3.66 m) from the body and is the distance at which we stand from strangers.

- *The public zone* has a range of over 12 feet (3.66 m) and is a comfortable distance from which to address a group of people.

The distance that would be acceptable in the training situation would correspond either to the 'social' or to the 'public zone'. Among the factors impacting upon the choice would be the physical nature of the room, the type of training and the nature of the task, the stage of the group's development and the personality of the learners and trainer(s). In determining distance and layout, a good rule of thumb is to choose what you feel comfortable with. Your comfort or anxieties will be projected on to the group, with a consequent positive or negative impact upon the learning process.

ACTIVE LISTENING

In the training situation, as in our working and everyday lives, we tend to believe that the better we are at talking, the better we shall be able to communicate. We tend to

▷ Table 3 Forms of communication

	Listening	Speaking	Reading	Writing
Learned	1st	2nd	3rd	4th
Used	Most (45%)	Next most (30%)	Next least (16%)	Least (9%)
Taught	Least	Next least	Next most	Most

give little attention to the listening part of the communication process, which is truly amazing when we consider the statistics given in Table 3.

Reproduced from *A Guide to Listening* (2nd impression, 1990) by Ian MacKay, British Association for Commercial and Industrial Education.

On average, people with normal learning abilities retain only 25 per cent of what they hear. There are many reasons why this is the case:

■ We perceive listening as a passive activity and find the prolonged concentration required impossible to maintain.

■ The average person speaks at about 130 words per minute, whereas our thinking speed is about 500 words per minute. Consequently, we are continually jumping ahead of what is actually being said. We often, therefore, go on 'mental walkabout', thinking of other things.

■ We don't clear our minds beforehand and so the 'noise in our system' shuts out or distorts what is being said.

■ The listener is tense with emotion so that his or her ability to listen is seriously impaired.

■ We are concerned with our reply so that the concentration is on this rather than what is being said to us.

■ The perception of the listener may so differ from the perception of the talker that a totally different and incorrect interpretation of the information may occur.

All of these factors can ensure that the message received is not the message sent. In some cases it may not bear even the slightest resemblance!

How can we improve our listening? Quite simply, by getting the receiver of the message (the learner) involved with the sender (the trainer). The communication becomes two-way so that the learner is involved in the learning process and the process of addressing and solving problems is improved.

The technique of making the process of communication two way is called *active listening*, and is an active not a passive process (see Figure 24 below). The steps in active listening are:

1   A sends a message.

2   B receives the message. This involves concentration and working out the implications of the message.

3   B states back what has been understood, but *makes no evaluations*.

4   A either agrees with B's interpretation or sends the message again if any misunderstanding has occurred.

5   The process is continually repeated, once understanding by both parties has been achieved.

Two techniques that can help us become more competent at active listening are 'summarising' and 'reflecting'.

Summarising

This is concerned with the factual side of the message and involves stating back to the speaker the listener's understanding of the information. Such paraphrasing should take place at regular intervals and has the advantages of:

- checking understanding

- offering an opportunity for clarification

- showing the speaker that you have been listening to what has been said, thus demonstrating your interest

- giving the speaker feedback on how well the message has been expressed.

Useful phrases are:

> 'As I understand it, what you're saying is . . .'
> 'So your point is that . . .'

Reflecting

Reflecting deals with the speaker's feelings, which may or may not be mentioned overtly. Such recognition of the speaker's feelings builds empathy between you. It enhances your understanding of the situation and of the person, and improves the communication process.

Useful phrases are:

> 'That must have made you very annoyed.'
> 'You felt that ...?'
> 'That must have been very satisfying for you.'

When reflecting, the listener acts as a mirror of the speaker's feelings, but does not pass comment or evaluate those feelings. Care must also be taken that our non-verbal signals – for example, tone of voice, facial expression – do not communicate a judgement of the speaker.

Active listening is most used in the counselling situation, often on a one-to-one basis. It is of benefit in the training situation – for example, when a learner is experiencing difficulty with the subject matter, when the learner disagrees with what the trainer has said, or when either wishes to clarify the content of a question.

Appropriately used, active listening can bring many benefits to the training situation.

- It shows the learners that you want to hear what they have to say. If you show people you are prepared to listen to them, they will be more willing to listen to you.

- It acknowledges the learners' presence and also their experience. Utilising their experience adds to the richness of learning for the group.

- It encourages a climate of openness and trust, and this improves communication.

- It helps the trainer tune in to individuals in the group and to recognise problems.

- It helps to break down learners' resistance by getting them more involved in the learning process.

- It recognises the importance of feelings in the communication process.

- It keeps the responsibility for learning and achieving solutions where it belongs – with the learner.

- It encourages a continuation and improvement in the communication process.

A comparison between active and passive listening is summarised in Figures 23 and 24.

TRANSACTIONAL ANALYSIS

Transactional Analysis (TA) is based on a theory of personality and communication, and provides a useful model for understanding and improving interpersonal relations and communication. It is a method of analysis to help an individual determine the basis from which another individual is communicating or interacting, and thus to decide how to

Figure 23 Passive listening

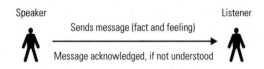

SPEAKER
- sends message
- receives the feedback on message and problem
- may be emotional
- may not be thinking very clearly
- receives little empathy or help

LISTENER
- finds concentration difficult
- has a cluttered mind
- is one jump ahead
- may be tense with emotion
- may be preoccupied by thinking about a reply
- may have a different perception

Result: little is communicated

Figure 24 Active listening

SPEAKER
- sends message
- receives feedback
- becomes relaxed
- is able to think more clearly
- feels the empathy of the listener
- is helped to solve problems
- feels better about self
- owns problem and solution
- makes commitment to solving problem

LISTENER
- has a clear mind
- interacts with speaker
- is relaxed
- does not make evaluations
- summarises facts
- reflects feelings
- helps the speaker to solve and own problems and solutions

Result: the quality of communication is vastly improved

respond. It is a valuable tool that can be used in all life situations in which we interact with others, as well as in the training situation.

The originator of TA was Eric Berne, a Canadian psychotherapist, who developed his theories during the 1950s. A number of concepts expressed in distinctive jargon are associated with TA, such as ego states, complementary, crossed and ulterior transactions, strokes, being OK/not OK, life scripts, games and tapes. These are all explained in this section.

Figure 25 The three ego states

TA implies that we communicate from different 'ego states', of which there are three. These three ego states are **P**arent, **A**dult and **C**hild (thus PAC), which are shown as three circles arranged vertically (see Figure 25). This diagram has become an internationally recognised symbol. Together, the three ego states form our personality which influences our behaviour throughout our lives. Although the ego states are usually arranged as in Figure 25, no hierarchical significance is attached.

Research has indicated that throughout life our brain is like a tape recorder that operates in two main modes – record and playback. We record our life experiences on three tapes – parent, adult and child – and the strongest recordings are usually those made during our early formative years or during a significant life event. These recordings are then stored in the brain to become part of our personality, and from time to time retrieved when we are subject to the right stimulus. We then make associations and we behave accordingly – ie the playback button is activated. When we hear a piece of music, see a film, or visit a place and it brings back good or bad memories – that's 'playback'.

No one operates constantly from the same role or state, and according to TA theory it is OK to assume any of the three roles if the circumstances warrant it. Usually, though, it is most appropriate and desirable to function in the adult role.

The ego states – basic structure

These represent the ways in which we react to our external world. In response to certain stimuli we may react in different ways – anxiety, fear, anger, enthusiasm – and each reaction reflects an underlying ego state. We may, in fact, have been programmed or conditioned to respond in such a way by our life experiences.

Parent ego state

This part of our personality is derived from observing, identifying with, and often imitating our parents or those who brought us up in our formative years. We often refer to them as *role models*. Teachers and relatives also play a significant part.

This state comprises a set of attitudes, values and behaviours that we have *learned*, consciously and unconsciously, from our role models in the past. We are acting from our parent ego state when we act in accordance with these attitudes, values and behaviours.

Adult ego state

When we operate from this ego state we are not conditioned by our past experiences. We operate from the here and now. This part of our personality is concerned with the acquisition and processing of information. Objectivity, analysis, rationality, logic, detachment, lack of emotional involvement and impartiality are some of the dispositions that characterise this ego state. It is this part of our personality, therefore, that we use in effective information processing, problem-solving and decision-making.

Child ego state

This is the part of our personality that we largely learned at an early age, usually the formative years up to the age of 7. In this ego state we are replaying behaviours, thoughts and/or feelings that we experienced in the past. We may reveal the child aspect of our personality in a number of ways – for example, by being creative, spontaneous, self-centred, stubborn, attention-seeking, cruel, by moaning, by throwing tantrums or by being self-indulgent. All of these are typical child-like behaviours that can, and do, surface in adult behaviour patterns.

Ego state functions

TA theorists believe that the basic structure of three ego states which constitute our personality can be further subdivided into five major functions. There are two within the Parent, one within the Adult and two within the Child. Diagrammatically, these five functions are shown in Figure 26.

Critical (or controlling) parent ego function

Parents spend a considerable amount of time controlling (and conditioning) the behaviour of their children. This is probably most obvious in the early years, although in some cases it may even accompany the child's progress into adulthood. Parents also

Figure 26 The major functions of ego states

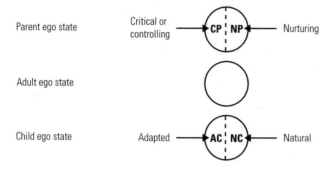

spend quite a lot of time criticising children's behaviour, because they want either to correct bad behaviour or to exercise control.

We have all experienced this, either as giver or receiver. In the organisational world this function would be most apparent in a bossy and directive manager, who may invite rebellion rather than obedience from peers, subordinates or trainees.

Nurturing parent ego function

Most of us have a caring side to our nature, and most of us will have been subject to a number of nurturing behaviours from our parents. It may have taken the form of being nursed through sickness, supported through a disappointment or through a stressful examination period, or simply by having a cuddle. We all need both to give and to receive care and attention from time to time, irrespective of age.

Adult ego function

This is the objective, rational, analytical, side of our personality that we use in a systematic way to solve problems and make decisions. Logic, rather than emotions, is the order of the day.

Staying perpetually in this function can make us appear cold, heartless, robotic and impersonal. While we might be effective in a problem-solving situation or doing a routine task efficiently, in a social situation we experience difficulties of familiarisation and limited friendship.

The natural child ego function

This is our natural state in which we enter the world and is concerned with our uninhibited show of natural feelings. Genuine displays of friendship, affection, excitement, sadness, contentment, frustration and curiosity emanate from this function. We are at our most natural and creative in this function, but if we display this ego function too frequently, we risk being labelled immature, adolescent, childish, naive, over-emotional and lacking in discipline.

The adapted child ego function

This function appears as a result of our conditioning at an early age. We learn that an uninhibited show of natural feelings is not always appropriate in the circumstances and so we adapt accordingly. We show we can behave correctly, often aware that such behaviour may have a pay-off for us in terms of a reward. For example, parental approval for good behaviour may result in the reward of sweets or that toy we have always wanted.

Adaptation begins at a very early age, and it is during this process that, in contrast with our uninhibited natural state, we are conditioned to learn feelings such as anxiety or guilt. Guilt about sex, learned in a repressive family environment, is a good example.

The PAC model and communication

TA as originally conceived by Berne focused mainly on the transactions between individuals. It was concerned with analysing the interaction between ego states of different persons.

Berne identified three main types of transaction, each with its own rules of communication.

Complementary transactions

A complementary transaction occurs when the ego state addressed is the ego state that responds. Two examples are shown in Figures 27 and 28.

Figure 27 Complementary transactions (1)

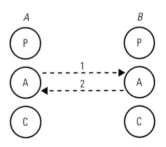

Person A speaks to the adult ego state and receives a reply from the adult ego state. The dialogue might be:

Person A: Have I explained that clearly to you?
Person B: Yes, it's fine. I now understand it.

Figure 28 Complementary transactions (2)

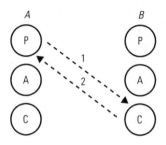

Person A speaks from the critical parent ego state to the child ego state, which responds accordingly. The dialogue might be:

Person A: You are making a terrible mess of that! I thought I'd shown you how to do it my way.
Person B: I thought I'd got the hang of it. Can you show me again?

Complementary transactions are OK, so interaction and communication usually continue.

Crossed transactions

A crossed transaction occurs when the ego state addressed is not the ego state that responds. Figures 29 and 30 illustrate two examples.

Crossed transactions are usually not OK and, before long, interaction and communication cease. They will resume when a re-matching of ego states has taken place. As trainers we can:

Figure 29 Crossed transactions (1)

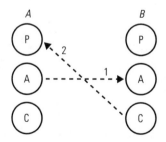

Here Person A speaks to the adult ego state and receives a response from the child ego state directed to the parent ego state. The dialogue might be:

Person A: There will be an examination on Friday.
Person B: Not another one! Well, I'm not prepared, so I shan't be turning up for it.

Figure 30 Crossed transactions (2)

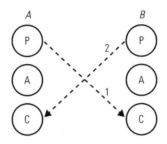

Here Person A speaks from the parent ego state addressing the child ego state and receives a response from the parent ego state addressing Person A's child ego state. The dialogue might be:

Person A: How many times have I told you to do it this way?
Person B: Well, if you were better at explaining it, I'd probably get the hang of it.

- choose which ego state we wish to communicate from – preferably the adult ego state

- consider the effect we want to have on our trainees before choosing the appropriate ego state.

Sometimes it can be appropriate to address an ego state other than the adult, such as the natural or adopted child. These latter two functions are present in all of us, and in the relaxed atmosphere of an off-site training event, far removed from the constraints of organisational life, communications that address the child ego states may, at times, be very appropriate.

Ulterior transactions

In most situations, relationships are usually characterised by complementary transactions. Often, however, relationships contain ulterior transactions in which there is a hidden message and the recipient must make use of his or her intuitive powers in order to pick up the full or real message. External or behavioural signals do not really convey the deeper message.

These transactions usually involve the use of two ego states simultaneously, and this category is the basis for playing games. The use of more than two ego states simultaneously is sometimes referred to as an *angular transaction*. Such transactions are not uncommon in organisational life, but should be uncommon occurrences in the training situation where, hopefully, a positive and trusting climate exists that is conducive to learning.

An example of an ulterior transaction is illustrated in Figure 31, where the overt message from Person A (manager) to Person B (subordinate) might be along the lines of 'I think your career would benefit from a new challenge,' or 'I think you would welcome a change.' The ulterior message, however, might be rather different: 'I think it is time you got on your bike and went somewhere else. You are not performing.'

Interacting with people skilled in the use of ulterior transactions is difficult, and unless the underlying concerns are brought into the open, harmonious and trusting relationships will not be established.

Strokes

Part of life's ritual involves collecting things, like stamps, and during our lifetime we collect numerous 'strokes' which, in TA terms, are *units of recognition*. The importance of strokes and the kind of strokes required varies according to our upbringing (conditioning) and our personality. In TA terms, its importance is determined by our life script.

There are three types of strokes:

Positive strokes

This is positive feedback, or 'warm fuzzies'. For example, after a training session the trainer might say, 'John, I really appreciated your contribution this morning.'

Positive strokes recognise effort, make us feel valued and secure, and increase self-esteem and confidence. In short, they make people feel good about themselves.

Negative strokes

This is negative feedback, and these are sometimes referred to as 'cold pricklies'. They might take the form of criticism, contempt or ridicule, and they have the opposite effect of positive strokes – they should generally be avoided.

Figure 31 Ulterior transactions

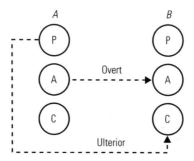

Negative feedback can be useful if delivered constructively, but careful attention should be given to *how* it is communicated.

Sometimes people indulge in playing a game of collecting negative strokes for which there is usually a pay-off for the person playing it – eg making a point, attracting attention, getting increased peer recognition. Try to avoid getting involved unless it is necessary.

No strokes

This is the most difficult situation to adapt to, and why solitary confinement is used as a severe punishment in penal establishments. A strokeless environment with no feedback at all reduces self-esteem, self-confidence and an individual's value to the group. It usually results in fall-out, demotivation and the playing of games to attract attention.

> **❝** Negative feedback is better than none. I would rather have a person hate me than overlook me. As long as he hates me, I make a difference. **❞**
> (M. Beattie)

Conclusion

Transactional Analysis has links with early learning theory and models of motivation. As a trainer, an in-depth knowledge and understanding of TA is not necessary. What is important is an awareness of your style and its impact upon an individual or a group. Some trainers who have unwittingly adopted an inappropriate critical parent style have often elicited adolescent behaviour from the recipients. Consequently, the focus of the course has been on playing negative games rather than on productive learning. This is one reason why those who have been in a training role and have adopted a 'schoolmaster' stance have frequently experienced problems in communicating with their learners. For the trainer, the main messages from TA are:

- We need to be aware of human conditioning and human needs.

- We need to be aware of our own mode of communication and to recognise the importance of communicating from our adult ego state.

- Recognition and feedback must be given regularly. Positive strokes develop self-esteem, increase motivation and enhance learning. Involving them, the training event does not become an arena for playing games, and time can be devoted to more positive outcomes.

EXERCISES

1   Consider two presenters you have observed: a good one, and one who needs to improve.
    (a)   Why were they good/poor?
    (b)   What did they actually do?
    (c)   What have you learned from your observations?

2   What are your strengths and weaknesses in communication? What can you do to improve your weaknesses? What opportunities are there for experimentation?

3   Ask a colleague to help you improve your skills in active listening. Remember, practice makes perfect.

4   Consider a number of interactive situations you have observed that demonstrate the principles of Transactional Analysis.
    (a)   What were those situations?
    (b)   What form of communication was used?
    (c)   What were the effects?
    (d)   What have you learned?
    (e)   What can you copy?

5   Think of a number of adults who regularly demonstrate one of the three different ego states. What effect did/do they have on people with whom they interact, including yourself? What can you learn from this?

6   Write a number of brief dialogues that demonstrate complementary, crossed and ulterior transactions.

KEY POINTS

Major points in this chapter include:

- Communication is a two-way process and it must be kept simple.

- We communicate far more non-verbally than we do verbally.

- Listening is an active process. It is the most used but least taught communication skill. We should regularly practise listening.

- According to Transactional Analysis (TA), we communicate from three different 'ego states' – parent, adult and child – and the adult-to-adult mode of communication is the best in most situations.

- TA emphasises yet again the importance of positive feedback ('warm fuzzies') as a motivating tool.

▌FURTHER READING

ARGYLE M. (1967) *The Psychology of Interpersonal Behaviour.* Harmondsworth, Penguin Books.

ARGYLE M. (1973) *Skills With People: A guide for managers.* London, Hutchinson.

BEATTIE M. (1989) *Beyond Co-dependency.* New York, Harper & Row.

BERNE E. (1964) *Games People Play. The Psychology of Human Relationships.* New York, Grove Press.

BERNE E. (1972/1975) *What Do You Say After You Say Hello?* New York, Grove Press; London, Corgi.

BIRDWHISTELL R. L. (1971) *Kinesis and Context.* London, Allen Lane.

FAST J. (1971) *Body Language.* London, Souvenir Press.

HARRIS T. A. (1973) *I'm OK – You're OK.* London, Jonathan Cape.

HAY J. (1992) *Transactional Analysis for Trainers.* Maidenhead, McGraw-Hill.

MACKAY I. (1998) *Listening Skills.* London, Chartered Institute of Personnel and Development.

MEHRABIAN A. (1969) *Tactics in Social Influence.* Englewood Cliffs, New Jersey, Prentice-Hall.

MEHRABIAN A. (1971) *Silent Messages.* Belmont, California, Wadsworth.

PEASE A. (1981) *Body Language. How to read others' thoughts by their gestures.* London, Sheldon Press.

WISMER J. N. (1978) 'Communication effectiveness: active listening and sending feeling messages', in PFEIFFER J. W. and JONES J. E. (eds) *The Annual Handbook for Group Facilitators.* Tucson, Arizona, University Associates.

9 ■ AUDIO-VISUAL AIDS

Audio-visual aids are powerful tools to help you improve your training and your delegates' learning. Competence in using them, and knowing when to use them, are some of the skills you must acquire.

After reading this chapter, you will:

- be familiar with the main types of audio-visual aid
- be able to list some of the main rules for their use
- know how to use them in a competent manner.

There are many times during a training event when your verbal message can be enhanced by the use of a teaching aid. Remember that the teaching aid is not a replacement tutor. Remember also, the more complex the aid, the more likely it is to go wrong and thus detract from your message.

Audio-visual aids should serve some of the following purposes:

- to highlight key points
- to illustrate complicated information
- to add variety
- to increase the attention span/concentration of the learner
- to reinforce the message.

Consequently they must be:

- short
- concise

- simple

- easy to read/hear.

TYPES

Audio-visual aids can be classified accordingly:

- Display aids
  - chalkboards
  - wall charts
  - posters
  - flipcharts
  - whiteboards

- Projected aids
  - overhead transparencies
  - graphics packages
  - films (and videos)
  - filmstrips
  - slides
  - epidiascopes

- Three-dimensional aids
  - actual objects
  - models
  - mock-ups

- Duplicated or printed aids
  - handouts
  - reading lists

- Visual displays
  - television
  - video disks/interactive video.

Audio aids are usually cassette recordings in their own right or an integral part of a visual aid, so that it becomes an audio-visual aid.

	Excellent	**Satisfactory**	**Room for improvement**
15 Uses a variety of learning methods.			
16 Gives clear and concise explanations and briefings.			
17 Relates well to his/her colleagues in the training team.			
18 During presentations: (a) structures them clearly (b) ensures that speech is clear and audible (c) uses appropriate body language (d) conveys enthusiasm (e) involves the group (f) makes good use of visual aids.			
19 Listens effectively and checks for understanding.			
20 Distributes handouts of appropriate quality.			
21 Gives the opportunity for feedback and evaluation.			
22 Establishes a good relationship with the host centre and the support staff			
23 Manages the whole event with an easy competence.			
24 Encourages experimentation and individual contributions.			
25 Values the group as people.			

Action plan

Some of the things I do well are:

Some of the things I need to improve on are:

What I shall do to ensure that I improve:

If you have used both the self-evaluation checklist and the facilitator evaluation checklist, compare the two. Check out your perceptions and then finalise your action plan.

Do not lose sight of all the things you do well. These you repeat and keep in your repertoire.

LEARNER EVALUATION

In the last section, the learners had an opportunity to evaluate the facilitator. They must also have the opportunity to evaluate the product – ie the course, workshop, etc – because their comments provide invaluable information not only on how the course met their needs but also on how the course can be improved for future participants. Such feedback is especially important with a new course, but should also be received with a well-established course – not just to guard against complacency and staleness but to check whether needs have changed. Training is a dynamic entity and can never stand still.

Below is a typical evaluation form. It can be used at the end of a training course, at the end of a major segment, or after one session if such a session is new or has been considerably revised. Do not use the form too often or you risk alienating your learners.

Learner's course evaluation

Course:	Name (optional):
Date:	Job title (optional):
	Trainer(s):

Directions: Below are a series of paired, opposing statements about various aspects of the course. Please respond to each pair by circling what you would consider the appropriate number from 1 to 5.

1	The course objectives were clearly explained.	5 4 3 2 1	The course objectives were not explained.	
2	The course objectives were consistent with my needs and abilities.	5 4 3 2 1	The course objectives were not consistent with my needs and abilities.	
3	The methods used were appropriate to meet course objectives.	5 4 3 2 1	The methods used were inappropriate to meet course objectives.	
4	The course was well structured.	5 4 3 2 1	The course was poorly structured.	
5	The course introduced me to a lot of new knowledge.	5 4 3 2 1	The course taught me nothing new.	
6	There was plenty of opportunity for reinforcement of learning.	5 4 3 2 1	There was no opportunity for reinforcement of learning.	
7	The course was appropriate for this group in terms of: (a) content (b) method.	 5 4 3 2 1 5 4 3 2 1	The course was inappropriate for this group in terms of: (a) content (b) method.	

8	I felt motivated to learn more.	5	4	3	2	1		I felt unmotivated to learn more.
9	The course content was closely related to objectives.	5	4	3	2	1		The course content was unrelated to objectives.
10	The visual aids were used well and assisted my learning.	5	4	3	2	1		The visual aids were used poorly and did not assist my learning.
11	The standard of presentation was high.	5	4	3	2	1		The standard of presentation was poor.
12	The course handouts were of a very high standard.	5	4	3	2	1		The course handouts were of a poor standard.
13	The course handouts reinforced my learning.	5	4	3	2	1		The course handouts did nothing to help my learning.
14	The atmosphere in the group was very conducive to learning.	5	4	3	2	1		The atmosphere in the group hindered my learning.
15	The tasks presented had practical relevance.	5	4	3	2	1		The tasks presented had no practical relevance.
16	I always felt my questions were fully answered.	5	4	3	2	1		I never felt my questions were answered.
17	I always felt I could contribute my experience.	5	4	3	2	1		I never felt I could contribute my experience.
18	The administrative arrangements were excellent and contributed to the success of the course.	5	4	3	2	1		The administrative arrangements were poor and made no positive contribution to the success of the course.
19	The training and/or conference facilities were excellent.	5	4	3	2	1		The training and/or conference facilities were poor.
20	The time allocation for the course was perfect.	5	4	3	2	1		The time allocation for the course was inappropriate.
21	The trainer(s) gave me the support I needed to learn.	5	4	3	2	1		The trainer(s) gave me little support to assist my learning.

22	Much of the learning can be taken away and applied.	5	4	3	2	1	I have learned nothing of relevance or practical application.

23	The most useful parts of the course were:

24	The least useful parts of the course were:

25	To improve the course further I would suggest the following:

Thank you for completing the form. Your comments are greatly appreciated.

Learning and action plans

On training courses it is important to keep at the back of the delegate's mind the real world and what learning he or she is going to transfer from the course.

A useful way of doing this, and of reinforcing learning, is to conduct a learning review at the end of each day. Delegates are asked to record on paper at least three things they have learned during the day and which are probably of use back in the real world. Delegates are then asked to share these with the rest of group.

This is a very useful process. It gives feedback on learning and progress on a daily basis to tutors and course members, and keeps the focus on transferring learning. As the course proceeds the delegates build up a large learning log, and this can then form the basis of their action plan.

The formal action plan is produced towards the end of the course from the learning log as follows:

1   Learning is grouped in a meaningful way.

2   Tasks are identified and prioritised.

3   Methods of implementation are considered.

4   A realistic time-frame is decided (usually no more than six months).

A very useful process at this stage is to institute a co-counselling network in which each participant can be helped by another course member either to finalise the action plan or simply just to share it and receive some kind of feedback. If the group has been together for a reasonable period of time and has matured, members should be very amenable to such a process and should learn from the experiences.

The action plan is a positive commitment on the part of each individual to post-course follow-up action. It also forms an excellent basis for follow-up, which could be either with the trainers (easier if they are internal) or with the sponsoring manager at work.

Trainers can discuss with a delegate and/or manager the extent to which the action plan has been implemented and why there has been success or failure. They can also receive feedback on the benefits to the organisation accruing from the action plan, and thus, indirectly, some indication of how the course met individual, departmental and organisational needs.

TESTING

A good proportion of training, particularly in the management development field, does not involve testing. In many other courses it is an important part of the proceedings. Tests have three main uses:

■   to evaluate the achievements of the delegates

■   to measure the effectiveness of the training in relation to your tuition

■   to locate errors and weaknesses that need correction.

In general, any test that you develop and/or use should be:

■   valid – ie should measure what it is supposed to measure

■   reliable – ie should consistently give the same result no matter who administers or scores it

■   usable in your situation.

Note: a test may be excellent, but if it takes too long to administer or is impossible to score with the measuring devices available, then it is not usable. It is part of your role to exercise sound, professional judgement about the best tool for the job.

Tests fall into two major categories:

- performance tests
- knowledge tests.

Performance tests

These measure skills. In its truest form, a performance test is a one-to-one situation in which the trainer carefully evaluates a single individual as a task or series of tasks is accomplished. Driving a car or flying an aircraft (on a simulator or for real) are good examples. It is an excellent way of finding out exactly what an individual can do – but it is very time-consuming if it has to be applied to each individual in the group.

Performance tests must be carefully planned. When preparing such a test you must ensure that you:

- determine exactly the elements you wish to test
- list the operations and/or steps
- establish acceptable standards for each element being tested, as well as the relative value of each element
- prepare instructions, preferably written
- develop a scoring sheet that will provide a standardised guide when observing and evaluating individuals
- list and have available all equipment needed to perform the test.

Knowledge tests

There are two main types of knowledge test: subjective and objective. The former is the essay-type test and is not often used in training situations, mainly because of problems of standardisation and gradings.

There are, however, several types of objective tests, and if you are going to use them you should:

- know exactly what it is you intend to teach, and the results you hope to achieve

- know the importance of the material you select for testing in relation to the overall course objectives – this involves working out the value or importance of the parts to the whole

- have prioritised the items selected for testing, giving them a proportionate part of the total test (so that the most important parts form a larger proportion of the test).

The various types of objective test are:

Oral

These are usually used for pre-testing or review, and their preparation requires the same attention to detail as a written test. In each case you need to determine in advance what the possible range of correct answers is for each question. You will then know how to react to what you hear or see.

Completion

These require individuals to finish a statement or drawing, and this type of test represents a compromise between the recall of an essay and the 50/50 chance of a good guess provided by the true–false question. Do not be surprised by the variety of correct answers you can get for questions that you were certain had only one answer. This is why there is a need to continually refine the questions. It is also why only tasks that require simple calculations or verbal associations should be tested with a completed question. Devising such questions may well cause you to concentrate on detail, so you should limit the use of this type of question to the testing of bits of information and specific facts.

Multiple-choice

A question on a multiple-choice test paper consists of an introductory query or incomplete statement with four or more suggested answers. The object is to choose the best or nearest-correct response. In this way you avoid the requirement of an answer that is absolutely true in all circumstances and reduce the opportunities for respondents to introduce different replies to those you are expecting. The guessing factor is considerably reduced with multiple-choice questioning, especially if four or five responses are provided. For a 10-item, four-response, multiple-choice test the probability of obtaining a score of 70 per cent on the basis of guesswork alone is 1 in 1,000. When this is coupled with a large sample of content, the multiple-choice test is a very useful test of knowledge.

Matching

A matching test usually consists of a list of questions, with a separate list comprising at least one possible answer to each question. The object is to choose an answer for each question. A lot of material can be covered with this type of test. The guessing factor is small and the scoring is simple and objective.

True–false

Such tests consist of statements to be judged true or false and answered accordingly (or with 'yes' or 'no'). A large number of items can be answered and scored in a short period of time, so a wide sampling of material is possible. When a scoring key is used, there is no difference of opinion on the correct answer and the scoring is speeded up.

True–false tests are useful for testing pieces of information and specific facts. The main problems are that:

- Very few statements can be made that can be answered with a definite 'true' or 'false', 'yes' or 'no'. Very few issues are black and white – there are usually shades of grey in between. Many subjects to be tested thus do not lend themselves to the true–false form of questioning.

- The questions have to be carefully written so that they are not misinterpreted.

- The chance of getting a correct answer through guessing is 50 per cent. On a 10-item true–false test the chance of answering 70 per cent of questions correctly through guesswork is 1 in 6.

All these types of test serve as a tool to help the trainer evaluate knowledge learning. Administering these tests is as much a test of your competence to impart knowledge as it is of your students' ability to assimilate knowledge.

Detailed information and advice on test design and construction is beyond the scope of this book. Your local reference library or the social sciences or education department library at your local university should have a wealth of information on this.

EXERCISES

1   List a number of courses in which you have been involved.
   (a)   What types of evaluation did you carry out?
   (b)   What were the outcomes?
   (c)   What aspects can be improved upon?
   (d)   What could you implement?

2 Have you ever received evaluations on yourself as a trainer? What feedback was positive? What areas do you need to work on to improve?

3 Are there any courses in which you will be involved in the future? If so, what type of evaluation will you carry out?

KEY POINTS

Major points in this chapter are:

- Evaluation is a constant process and is the fifth stage in the training cycle.

- Evaluation can help you improve your own competence as a trainer as well as improve the quality of a course.

- Learning reviews and action planning reinforce learning, increase the likelihood of transfer of learning, and give further information on the effectiveness of training.

- Testing is a useful method of evaluating student learning as well as your ability to impart relevant knowledge and train in appropriate skills.

- There are many types of objective tests suitable for evaluating learning.

FURTHER READING

BARTRAM S. and GIBSON B. (1999) *Evaluating Training*. Aldershot, Gower.

BEE F. and BEE R. (2003) *Learning Needs Analysis and Evaluation*. London, Chartered Institute of Personnel and Development.

BRAMLEY P. (1996) *Evaluating Training*. London, Chartered Institute of Personnel and Development.

EASTERBY-SMITH M. (1994) *Evaluating Management Developments, Training and Education*. 2nd edition. Aldershot, Gower.

GOLDSTEIN I. L. (1980) 'Training in work organisation', *Annual Review of Psychology*, pp.220–272.

HOLCOMB J. (1998) *Training Evaluation Made Easy: Make your training worth every penny*. London, Kogan Page.

NEWBY A. C. (1992) *Training Evaluation Handbook*. Aldershot, Gower.

REAY D. (1994) *Evaluating Training*. London, Kogan Page.

APPENDIX: BEYOND THIS BOOK

A book should not be an end in itself. Although it should increase your knowledge, its main contribution should be in helping you put into practice your learning. Keep your own situation to the forefront of your mind – only *you* can do that, and only *you* can implement your learning, but both *you and others* benefit from this process.

Here are a number of ways/suggestions to help you implement your learning. This is a suggested framework only, so feel free to adopt and change it in any way that suits you.

Part 1

1 Major learning points for me from this book include:

....

....

2 Some of the learning points that I could implement are:

....

....

3 In order of priority, the learning points I am going to implement are:

....

....

4 For each action point on my list, I must now decide:

Action point	*How I am going to implement it*	*When I am going to implement it*

....

....

....

To help me action these points, I may need to answer the following questions:

1   The factors that will help me are:

....

....

2   The factors that will hinder me are:

....

....

3   The kind of supports I need are:

....

....

4   The people from whom I want these supports are:

....

....

GOOD LUCK!

Now here are 12 suggested activities to help you develop as a trainer. Some of them could be integrated into Part 1.

Part 2

1   Be aware of my strengths but recognise that I never stop learning.

2   Experiment with one new method on my next course.

3   Introduce at least one new element into a course every time I deliver it.

4   Take the opportunity to observe someone else in the training situation.

5   Take the opportunity to co-facilitate with different people.

6   Make a contract with myself and my boss for a number of days for personal development every year. (Remember that going on a course gives you insight into what it is like on the other side of the desk.)

7   Join a reference group of practitioners in the same field – locally or nationally – and discuss my work and hear about theirs.

8   Be aware of the literature in my field and continually update. Read one new book every three months.

9 Subscribe to relevant journals in my field, and read them.

10 Draw up a learning log to record my observations and learning after
   (a) every session
   (b) every training day
   (c) every training course.

   With every learning point, consider how and when you can implement it. Use the guide in Part 1 of this Appendix if appropriate.

11 Write about my own experiences and share them with others.

12 Give of myself unselfishly in all situations – that usually guarantees I shall get more back!

BIBLIOGRAPHY

ALDER H. (1993) *The Right Brain Manager*. London, Piatkus.

ALDER H. (1994) *NLP: The New Art and Science of Getting What You Want*. London, Piatkus.

ALDERFER C. P. (1972) *Existence, Relatedness and Growth*. New York, Free Press.

AMERICAN SOCIETY FOR TRAINING AND DEVELOPMENT (1994) *The Past, Present and Future of Workplace Learning*. Alexandria, Virginia, American Society for Training and Development.

ARGYLE M. (1967) *The Psychology of Interpersonal Behaviour*. Harmondsworth, Penguin Books.

ARGYLE M. (1973) *Skills With People: A guide for managers*. London, Hutchinson.

BANK J. (1994) *Outdoor Development for Managers*. 2nd edition. Aldershot, Gower.

BANDLER R. and GRINDER J. (1979) *Frogs into Princes*. London, Real People Press.

BARTRAM S. and GIBSON B. (1994) *Activities for Developing Training Skills*. Aldershot, Gower.

BARTRAM S. and GIBSON B. (1997) *Training Needs Analysis*. 2nd edition. Aldershot, Gower.

BARTRAM S. and GIBSON B. (1999) *Evaluating Training*. Aldershot, Gower.

BEARD C. and WILSON J. P. (2001) *The Power of Experiential Learning: A handbook for trainers and educators*. Aldershot, Gower.

BEATTIE M. (1989) *Beyond Co-dependency*. New York, Harper & Row.

BEE F. and BEE R. (2003) *Learning Needs Analysis and Evaluation*. London, Chartered Institute of Personnel and Development.

BEE F. and BEE R. (1998) *Facilitation Skills*. London, Chartered Institute of Personnel and Development.

BERNE E. (1964) *Games People Play: The psychology of human relationships*. New York, Grove Press.

BERNE E. (1972/1975) *What Do You Say After You Say Hello?* New York, Grove Press; London, Corgi.

BIRDWHISTELL R. L. (1971) *Kinesis and Context*. London, Allen Lane.

BRAMLEY P. (1996) *Evaluating Training*. London, Chartered Institute of Personnel and Development.

BUCKLEY R. and CAPLE J. (2000) *The Theory and Practice of Training*. 4th edition. London, Kogan Page.

CAMERON E. (2001) *Facilitation Made Easy: Practical Tips to Improve Meetings and Workshops*. 2nd edition. London, Kogan Page.

CHARTERED INSTITUTE OF PERSONNEL AND DEVELOPMENT (2003) *5th Annual Training Survey*. London, CIPD.

CLARKE A. (2001) *Designing Computer-Based Learning Materials*. Aldershot, Gower.

CONSTABLE J. and McCORMICK R. (1987) *The Making of British Managers*. London, BIM and CBI.

COOPERS and LYBRAND ASSOCIATES (1985) *Challenge to Complacency*. Sheffield, MSC, November.

COUPLAND D. (1994) *Generation X*. Abacus, London.

DALE H. C. (1968) 'Memory and effective instruction', *Aspects of Education*, 7, 8–21.

DILTS R. (1983) *Applications of Neuro-Linguistic Programming*. Cupertino, California, Meta Publications.

DOUGLAS T. (1983) *Groups – Understanding People Gathered Together*. London and New York, Tavistock.

EASTERBY-SMITH M. (1994) *Evaluating Management Developments, Training and Education*. 2nd edition. Aldershot, Gower.

ELLINGTON H., FOWLIE J. and GORDON M. (1998) *Using Games and Simulations in the Classroom*. London, Kogan Page.

FAST J. (1971) *Body Language*. London, Souvenir Press.

GOLDSTEIN I. L. (1980) 'Training in work organisation', *Annual Review of Psychology*, pp.220–272.

HACKETT P. (1997) *Introduction To Training*. London, Chartered Institute of Personnel and Development.

HANDY C., GORDON C., GOW I., MALONEY M. and RANDLESOME C. (1987) *The Making of Managers: A report on management education, training and development in USA, West Germany, France, Japan and the UK*. London, NEDO, MSC and BIM.

HARDINGHAM A. (1996) *Designing Training*. London, Chartered Institute of Personnel and Development.

HARRIS T. A. (1973) *I'm OK – You're OK*. London, Jonathan Cape.

HARRIS T. L. and SCHWANN W. E. (1961) *Selected Readings on the Learning Process*. New York, Oxford University Press.

HART L. B. (1996) *Icebreakers 3. Icebreakers, Links and Energisers*. Aldershot, Gower.

HAY J. (1992) *Transactional Analysis for Trainers*. Maidenhead, McGraw-Hill.

HEIDER J. (1986) *The Tao of Leadership*. Aldershot, Wildwood House.

HERON J. (1999) *The Complete Facilitator's Handbook*. London, Kogan Page.

HERON J. (1993) *Group Facilitation: Theories and models for practice*. London, Kogan Page.

HERTZBERG F. (1966) *Work and the Nature of Man*. Cleveland, Ohio, World Publishing.

HILLS H. (1999) *Team Based Learning*. Aldershot, Gower.

HOGAN C. (2003) *Practical Facilitation: A toolkit of techniques*. London, Kogan Page.

HOGAN C. (2002) *Understanding Facilitation:Theory and principle*. London, Kogan Page.

HOLCOMB J. (1998) *Training Evaluation Made Easy. Make Your Training Worth Every Penny*. London, Kogan Page.

HONEY P. and MUMFORD A. (1982) *A Manual of Learning Styles*. Maidenhead, Peter Honey.

HONEY P. and MUMFORD A. (1986) *Using Your Learning Styles.* 2nd edition. Maidenhead, Peter Honey.

HUNTER D., BAILEY A. and TAYLOR B. (1999) *Handling Groups in Action.* Aldershot, Gower.

INGLIS S. (1994) *Making the Most of Action Learning.* Aldershot, Gower.

JACQUES D. (1991) *Learning In Groups.* 2nd edition. London, Kogan Page.

JONES J. E. (1980) 'Dealing with disruptive individuals in meetings', in PFEIFFER J. W. and JONES J. E. (eds) *The 1980 Annual Handbook for Group Facilitators.* Tucson, Arizona, University Associates.

JONES K. (1995) *Icebreakers. A Source of Games, Exercises, and Simulations.* 2nd edition. Aldershot, Gower.

JONES K. (1997) *Games and Simulations Made Easy. Practical Tips To Improve Learning Through Gaming.* London, Kogan Page.

JONES K. (1989) *A Sourcebook of Management Simulations.* London, Kogan Page.

KIRBY A. (1992) *Games for Trainers* (Vols. 1 and 2). Aldershot, Gower.

KIRBY A. (1993) *Icebreakers 1.* Aldershot, Gower.

KIRBY A. (1994) *Games for Trainers* (Vol. 3). Aldershot, Gower.

KNOWLES H. and KNOWLES M. (1972) *Introduction to Group Dynamics.* 2nd edition. Chicago, Association Press/Follett.

KNOWLES M. S. (1975) *Self-Directed Learning.* Chicago, Association Press/Follett.

KNOWLES M. S. (1980) *The Modern Practice of Adult Education: From pedagogy to andragogy.* Chicago, Follett.

KNOWLES M. S. (1984) *The Adult Learner: A neglected species.* 3rd edition. Texas, Gulf Publishing.

KOHLER W. (1973) *The Mentality of Apes.* International Library of Psychology. London, Routledge.

KOLB D. A. (1984) *Experiential Learning.* Englewood Cliffs, New Jersey, Prentice Hall.

KOLB D. A. and FRY R. (1975) 'Towards an applied theory of experiential learning', in COOPER C. L. (ed.) *Theories of Group Process.* New York, Wiley.

LAO TZU (1980) *The Way of Life* (trans. Witter Bynner). New York, Perigee Books.

LEATHERMAN D. (1996) *Designing Training Programmes.* Aldershot, Gower.

LEIGH D. (1991) *A Practical Approach to Group Training.* London, Kogan Page.

MASLOW A. H. (1954) *Motivation and Personality.* 2nd edition. New York, Harper & Row.

McCLELLAND D., ATKINSON J. W., CLARKE R. A. and LOWELL F. A. (1976) *The Achievement Motive.* New York, Irvington.

McGREGOR D. C. (1960) *The Human Side of Enterprise.* New York, McGraw-Hill.

MEHRABIAN A. (1969) *Tactics in Social Influence.* Englewood Cliffs, New Jersey, Prentice-Hall.

MEHRABIAN A. (1971) *Silent Messages.* Belmont, California, Wadsworth.

MENTS M. V. (1999) *The Effective Use of Role Play. Practical Techniques For Improving Learning.* 2nd edition. London, Gower.

MUMFORD A. (1980) *Making Experience Pay.* Maidenhead, McGraw-Hill.

MUMFORD A. (1986) 'Learning to learn for managers', *Journal of European Industrial Training.* Vol. 10, No. 2. Bradford, MCB University Press.

MACKAY I. (1998) *Listening Skills.* London, Chartered Institute of Personnel and Development.

MALONE S. (2003) *Learning About Learning.* London, Chartered Institute of Personnel and Development.

McGILL I. and BEATY L. (1992) *Action Learning: A practitioner's guide.* London, Kogan Page.

MEGGINSON D. and PEDLER M. (1992) *Self Development: A facilitator's guide.* Maidenhead, McGraw-Hill.

NEWBY A. C. (1992) *Training Evaluation Handbook.* Aldershot, Gower.

NEWSTON J. W. and SCANNEL E. (1980) *Games Trainers Play: Experiential learning exercises.* San Francisco, McGraw-Hill.

O'CONNOR J. and SEYMOUR J. (2002) *Introducing Neurolinguistic Programming.* London, HarperCollins.

ORRIDGE M. (1998) *How To Deliver Training.* Aldershot, Gower.

PEASE A. (1981) *Body Language. How to Read Others' Thoughts by their Gestures.* London, Sheldon Press.

PEDLER M. (1991) *Action Learning in Practice.* 2nd edition. Aldershot, Gower.

PETERSEN R. (1998) *Training Needs Assessment in the Workplace.* 2nd edition. London, Kogan Page.

PFEIFER J.W. and JONES J. G. (eds) (1972 – 1981) *The Annual Handbook for Group Facilitators.* San Francisco, Pfeiffer (an imprint of John Wiley and Sons)

PFEIFER J.W. and JONES J. G. (eds) (1982 – 1983) *The Annual for Facilitators, Trainers and Consultants.* San Francisco, Pfeiffer (an imprint of John Wiley and Sons)

PFEIFER J.W. and JONES J. G. (eds) (1984 – 1994) *The Annual: Developing Human Resources.* San Francisco, Pfeiffer (an imprint of John Wiley and Sons)

PONT T. (1994) 'The role of the management development specialist', in MUMFORD A. (ed.) *Handbook of Management Development.* 4th edition. Aldershot, Gower.

PONT T. (1995) *Investing in Training and Development: Turning interest into capital.* London, Kogan Page.

PONT G. and PONT T. (1998) *Interviewing Skills for Managers.* London, Piatkus.

PORTER M. (2003) *UK Competitiveness: Moving to the next stage.* London, Department of Trade and Industry.

POWELL L. (1980) *A Guide to the Overhead Projector.* 3rd edition. London. British Association for Commercial and Industrial Education.

RAE L. (1992) *A Guide to In-Company Training Methods.* Aldershot, Gower.

RAE L. (1997) *Planning and Designing Training Programmes.* Aldershot, Gower.

RAE L. (1997) *Using Presentations in Training and Development.* Aldershot, Gower.

RAE L. (1998) *Using Training Aids in Training and Development.* Aldershot, Gower.

REAY D. (1994) *Evaluating Training.* London, Kogan Page.

REID M.A., BARRINGTON H. and KENNEY J. (1999) *Training Interventions: Promoting learning opportunities.* 6th edition. London, Chartered Institute of Personnel and Development.

REVANS R. W. (1971) *Developing Effective Managers.* Harlow, Longman.

REVANS R. W. (1982) *The Origins and Growth of Action Learning.* Bromley, Chartwell Bratt.

REVANS R. W. (1983) *ABC of Action Learning,* Bromley, Chartwell Bratt.

ROBERTS-PHELPS G. (1998) *Flip Chart Games For Trainers.* Aldershot, Gower.

ROBSON M. (1995) *Facilitating.* Aldershot, Gower.

ROGERS C. (1983) *Freedom to Learn.* Columbus, Ohio, Merrill.

ROSE C. (1991) *Accelerated Learning.* Aylesbury, Accelerated Learning Systems.

RUSSELL T. (1998) *Effective Feedback Skills.* 2nd edition. London, Kogan Page.

SIDDONS S. (1997) *Delivering Training.* London, Chartered Institute of Personnel and Development.

SKINNER B. F. (1953) *Science and Human Behaviour.* New York, Macmillan.

SKINNER B. F. (1972) *Beyond Freedom and Dignity.* New York, Knopf.

SLOMAN M. (2001) *The E-Learning Revolution: From propositions to action.* London, Chartered Institute of Personnel and Development.

STIMSON N. (2002) *How to Write and Prepare Training Materials.* 2nd edition. London, Kogan Page.

THORNE K. (2002) *Blended Learning. How to Integrate Online and Traditional Learning.* London, Kogan Page.

TOUGH A. (1979) *The Adults' Learning Projects. A Fresh Approach to Theory and Practice.* 2nd edition. Toronto, Ontario, The Ontario Institute for Studies in Education.

UNIVERSITY ASSOCIATES (1983) *Encyclopaedia of Icebreakers.* Tucson, Arizona, University Associates.

VROOM V. H. (1964) *Work and Motivation.* New York, Wiley.

WEINSTEIN K. (1998) *Action Learning: A practical guide.* 2nd edition. Aldershot, Gower.

WILSON D. (2003) *Building the E-Learning Organisation.* London, Chartered Institute of Personnel and Development.

WISMER J. N. (1978) 'Communication effectiveness: active listening and sending feeling messages', in PFEIFFER J. W. and JONES J. E. (eds) *The Annual Handbook for Group Facilitators.* Tucson, Arizona, University Associates.

YERKES R. M. and DODSON J. D. (1908) 'The relation of strength of stimulus to rapidity of habit formation', *Journal of Comparative Neurological Psychology*, 18, 459–82.

INDEX